DATE DUE

	OCT 27 1984		
MAR 25 1986			
JAN	3 1989		
NOV 2 3 1991			
MAR 1 6 1993			
DEC 2 1 1993			
DEC 1 8 1995			
APR 1 3 2004			

DEMCO NO. 38-298

7310032

Brazil

Series Editor Lesley Firth
Edited by Julia Kirk
Design Peter Benoist
Picture Research Elizabeth Ogilvie
Production Rosemary Bishop
Consultant John Howard
Illustrations Ron Hayward Associates
John Shackell
Maps Matthews & Taylor Associates

Photographic sources Key to positions of illustrations: *(T)* top, *(C)* centre, *(B)* bottom, *(L)* left, *(R)* right, *(M)* middle. AAA *23(BR)*. American History Library *28(TL)*, *29(M)*. BBC *51(TL)*. Bodleian Library *27(TR)*. Douglas Botting *11(BR)*, *20,32(TL)*, *34(BR)*, *41(TL,BR)*, *43(BR)*. Brazilian Embassy *9(BR)*, *13(ML)*, *15(BL)*, *23(TL,BL)*, *41(TR)*, *44(BR)*, *47(BL)*, *48(BR)*, *51(BL)*, *53(TL,BR)*. Mary Evans *26(BR)*. Rodolpho Machado *45(TR)*, *51(TR)*. Dennis Moore *9(TL, BL,TR)*, *10(TR)*, *11(TL,BL)*, *12(L,BR)*, *13(TL,BL,TR)*, *14(TL)*, *15(TL,TR)*, *16(T)*, *17(BL,TR,BR)*, *18(BL,BR)*, *19(TL,TR,B)*, *21(ML,BR)*, *22(BL)*, *24(TL,BL)*, *33(TL)*, *36(T)*, *39(TL,TR)*, *42(TR,B)*, *43(TL,BL,TR)*, *44(L)*, *46(TL)*, *47(TR)*, *48(TL)*, *49(BR)*, *51(BR)*, *53(M,BL)*. Peter Myers *14(BL)*. Museu de Arte, Sao Paulo *46(TR)*. Photri *35(TR)*. Popperfoto *30(TL,BR)*, *31(TR,ML,BR)*, *50(TR)*. Radio Times Hulton Picture Library *29(T,B)*, *47(BR)*. Snark International *27(BR)*, *28(B)*. Varig Airlines *23(TR)*, *33(TR)*, *34(TL)*, *35(BL)*. Zefa *10(BL)*, *21(BL,TR)*, *22(TR)*, *25(BR)*, *33(BR)*, *37(TR,BL)*, *47(MB)*, *49(BR)*, *50(BR)*, *53(TR)*.

First published 1977
Macdonald Educational Ltd.
Holywell House, Worship Street
London EC2A 2EN

© Macdonald Educational
Limited 1977

ISBN 0 382-06182 9

Published in the United States by Silver Burdett Company, Morristown, N.J. 1978 Printing

Library of Congress
Catalog Card No. 78-56592

Endpaper: the colourful market at Manaus, on the River Negro. Tropical produce from the surrounding area is brought downriver and into the city by boat.

Page 6: merrymakers at the annual Carnival in Rio de Janeiro, where competitions are held to judge the best samba teams and the most original costumes.

Brazil

the land and its people

Ritchie Perry

Macdonald Educational

Contents

Land of many faces

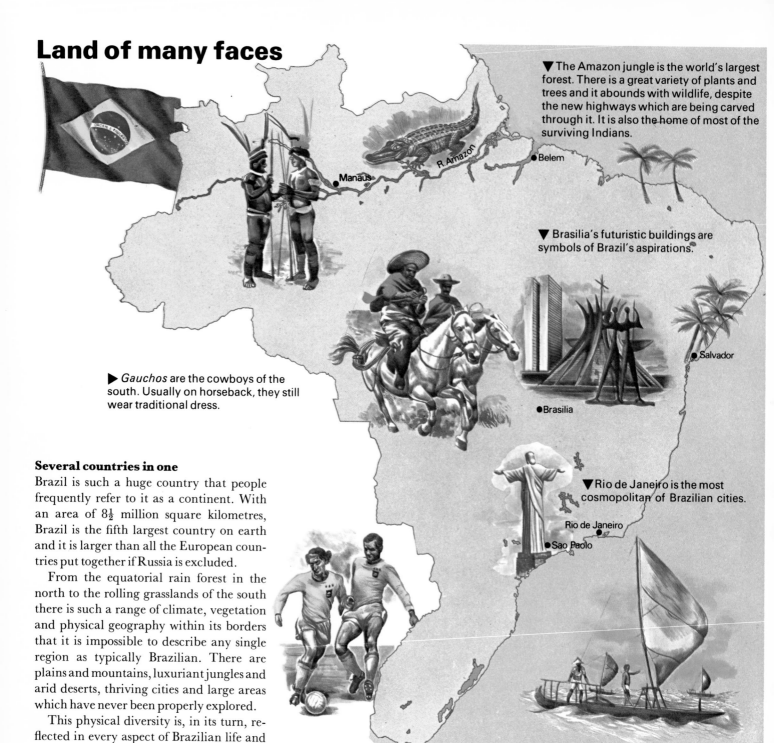

▼ The Amazon jungle is the world's largest forest. There is a great variety of plants and trees and it abounds with wildlife, despite the new highways which are being carved through it. It is also the home of most of the surviving Indians.

R. Amazon

● Belem

● Manaus

▼ Brasilia's futuristic buildings are symbols of Brazil's aspirations.

● Salvador

▶ *Gauchos* are the cowboys of the south. Usually on horseback, they still wear traditional dress.

● Brasilia

▼ Rio de Janeiro is the most cosmopolitan of Brazilian cities.

Rio de Janeiro ●

● Sao Paolo

▲ For many people football is almost as important as food or drink.

▲ The graceful but flimsy *jangadas* are used by the fishermen of the north-east.

Several countries in one

Brazil is such a huge country that people frequently refer to it as a continent. With an area of 8½ million square kilometres, Brazil is the fifth largest country on earth and it is larger than all the European countries put together if Russia is excluded.

From the equatorial rain forest in the north to the rolling grasslands of the south there is such a range of climate, vegetation and physical geography within its borders that it is impossible to describe any single region as typically Brazilian. There are plains and mountains, luxuriant jungles and arid deserts, thriving cities and large areas which have never been properly explored.

This physical diversity is, in its turn, reflected in every aspect of Brazilian life and each separate area has its own sense of identity. Within its borders can be found as many different Brazils as there are regions, all of them fused together to form a united country which dominates South America.

Old and new

Everywhere you go in Brazil the past is constantly rubbing shoulders with the present. Elegant colonial churches stand in the shadow of gleaming skyscrapers constructed of glass and steel. City dwellers dine in comfortable restaurants while *gauchos* and *vaqueiros* cook their meals over open fires. Cars throng the streets and highways while ox-carts and dug-out canoes are the main means of transport in parts of the interior.

Bustling cities

Most of the population lives on or near the coast where there are cities like Sao Paulo, Rio de Janeiro, Recife and a score of others with their pollution, traffic congestion and slums. However, the old Brazil is never very far away. The bustling metropolis of Sao Paulo is the largest industrial centre in Latin America. Only an hour or two's flying time away there are Indians who are still living in the stone age.

Inevitably, there is yet another contrast – the gulf between rich and poor. The appalling poverty of the slums and parts of the interior is a far cry from the opulence of the business sections of the major cities.

▲ Salvador was Brazil's first capital. Unlike other cities, it has managed to retain its colonial flavour.

► Many Brazilians live in abject poverty with few of the amenities of modern life, and often in remote settlements like this.

▲ With so many miles of tropical, palm fringed sand it is hardly surprising that going to the beach is almost a cult. The beaches are the country's major leisure attraction but it is always possible to find a secluded section of sand.

► Seen from the air, Sao Paulo's lack of planning makes it look as though a child had flung his bricks to the ground in a temper. It is Brazil's largest city.

An ethnic melting pot

A mixture of races

In some ways Brazil is very like the United States. As in America, Brazil has become a melting pot of cultures and races while the Indians, who were the original inhabitants, only form a minute proportion of the population today.

This ethnic mix is readily apparent on any busy street corner, for the passers-by will represent almost every shade of colour, from blackest black to whitest white. The process began in colonial days when the Portuguese inter-bred with Indians and Negro slaves. Successive waves of immigrants from Europe, the Middle East and Japan were similarly absorbed into the community.

Today Brazil is a truly multi-racial society where colour prejudice is at a minimum. However, the varied origins of the present population are still clearly visible. Large areas of the south display a marked Germanic influence and descendants of Italian immigrants are prominent in many cities and in the wine-growing area around Caxias. Sao Paulo has its own Japanese community and Salvador remains the "African" capital of Brazil.

The Portuguese influence

Much of the credit for Brazil becoming

▲ The few remaining Indians mainly live in scattered tribes in the Mato Grosso and Amazon basin.

▲ It was the Portuguese who created modern Brazil and provided the new nation with its language.

such a united country must go to the Portuguese settlers, who did far more than provide the national language. From the beginning they adopted a tolerant attitude towards their new-found citizens. Slaves were treated more as members of the family than as possessions. Children of Indian and Negro women were usually given full acknowledgement.

Most modern Brazilians are proud of their mixed ancestry. Brazil's success in absorbing all the varied elements in its population sets an example to the rest of the world. Poverty and illiteracy still have to be conquered but there is no discrimination against race, and little against colour.

▲ There are a few Japanese settlements in Parana but most of them are in or around Sao Paulo. As the photograph shows, they have taken over an entire section of the city and converted it into a self-contained community.

◀ Contact with civilization has had a disastrous effect on most Indian tribes and only a few of them still maintain their old way of life. Until they came into contact with the settlers they lived mainly by hunting and fishing. The use of iron was unknown to them.

▲ Descendants of the original slaves have left a deep mark on Brazilian society and its culture.

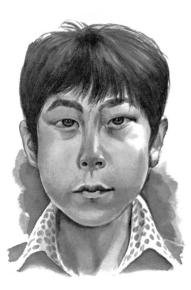

▲ Relatively few in number, the Japanese are the most tightly-knit of all the ethnic groups.

▲ The German settlers brought with them their native virtues of thrift, industry and business skill.

▲ Despite the lack of discrimination, the Negroes have not completely overcome their slave heritage.

◀ Nearly 60 per cent of the population is urban but each town and city has a flavour of its own. Settlers from so many different parts of the world have contributed to the creation of Brazil that it is often difficult to trace the origins of Brazilian characteristics.

▲ Many Italian immigrants settled in the south of Brazil as cattle ranchers, small landowners and shopkeepers. Most of them, however, went to Sao Paulo where they worked on the coffee plantations. They are also numerous in Rio Grande do Sul.

Family life

Children everywhere

There is a popular saying that there are two kinds of shop which hardly ever fail in Brazil – those selling toys and those selling baby clothes. Children and babies seem to be everywhere and the Brazilian love of children probably has some connection with the high infant mortality rate. Even today, so many children die at birth or in their infancy that those who do survive become doubly precious to their parents.

Large families are the rule rather than the exception throughout the country and more than half the population is under 19 years of age. Families of 20 are not uncommon and the average household contains four or five children.

Although the children are brought up fairly strictly, with great emphasis being placed on good manners, nothing is considered too good for them. Brazilian mothers seize every opportunity to dress up their offspring, and the children's costume balls are now a regular feature of Carnival.

Family ties

Even when the children have grown up into adults themselves, family ties remain as strong as ever. Respect for parents and grandparents is an enduring aspect of Brazilian life. Where possible, family get-togethers are a regular occurrence and several generations of the same family often assemble both at weekends and on important feast days. Members of a Brazilian family never lose touch with one another, wherever they might be.

A man's world

There can never be any doubt about who is the head of a Brazilian household. Old attitudes may be changing, but family life continues to revolve around the father. If he should die, his place as the breadwinner for the family would probably be taken by the eldest son.

So far Women's Lib has made no real impact in Brazil and it is only very recently that women have begun to think about careers for themselves. Relatively few worthwhile jobs are open to them, and many men resent the competition.

Most women still marry young, often at 17 or 18, and afterwards they are expected to devote the rest of their lives to their husbands and children. Wives do not yet have full legal rights and they are frequently content to think as their husbands do. Although there are signs that women are gradually becoming more emancipated, it will be many years before they are considered the equals of their menfolk.

Help in the home

Many Brazilian women do have some compensation for their inferior status. Maids' salaries are low and most middle and upper class families can afford to employ one. Since these maids do most of the cleaning, cooking and washing, and often help to take care of the children as well, housewives frequently have plenty of spare time on their hands. This probably accounts for the large number of hairdressing and beauty salons to be found in Brazilian cities.

▼ Washing machines are only for the well-to-do. More traditional methods have to suffice for the poorer sections of the community and such a scene is by no means uncommon in parts of the interior. Even in the towns and cities, washerwomen often take the place of laundries and do the weekly washing for the more affluent households.

▶ As Brazilian cities become larger, so do the suburbs surrounding them. Most city-dwellers live in apartments but there are few families who do not aspire to owning a house of their own, like this Japanese family.

▲ There are few career opportunities for women. Maids are expected to work hard and wages are usually low.

▲ This is a typical better-class home. The tropical climate makes shutters essential for all Brazilian houses.

◀ In wealthier households a nanny may look after the children. She may even be employed exclusively for this purpose. Such close contact makes the children treat her as a member of the family and she may stay long after the children have all grown up.

▼ Every town has its parks and many of them include a children's playground. Parks are used by people of all classes and, where there is no nearby beach, they are favourite spots for a family outing. The cool shade of the park is a welcome relief from the city's heat.

Family timetable

6·30 a.m.

7–8 a.m.

8·30 a.m.

8·30 a.m.

Mid-morning

12·30–1·00

12·30–1·00

12·30–1·00

12·30–1·00

Mid-afternoon

4·00 p.m.

6–7 p.m.

7·30–8·00 p.m.

9·00 p.m.

Midnight

Shopping Brazilian style

▼ One market with a difference can be found at Manaus. Tropical produce from smallholdings in the surrounding area is brought down the Rio Negro and into the city by boat and then sold directly to customers. Shopping attains another dimension when customers risk a soaking in the river!

Shops for everyone

Brazilian shops cater for everybody. Roadside vendors offer their wares on the pavements and beside the main highways, every street boasts its neighbourhood shop and all the cities have their supermarkets.

Much of the shopping is done daily, as Brazilian housewives prefer to buy their food fresh rather than frozen and prepackaged, especially meat and fish. Bread and pastries can be bought straight from the baker's oven.

Most small shops open early in the morning and do not close until late at night. Although there are many shops selling the latest fashions, clothes are expensive and a lot of women either make their own or employ a dressmaker. The best bargains are the precious stones which Brazil produces in such abundance.

The feiras

The colourful *feiras*, or street markets, are a feature of every town and city. In the larger markets customers can buy just about everything, from caged songbirds to local craftwork and Indian bows and arrows. Mainly, however, they sell fresh vegetables, fruit, eggs and flowers.

Many of the stalls are a riot of colour, particularly those selling fruit. Mounds of pineapples, oranges, water melons, avocados and tomatoes mingle with more exotic fruits such as persimmons, passion fruit and japoticaba. One whole stall may be given over to the different kinds of banana. There is such a galaxy of choice that the main problem facing the shoppers is deciding exactly what they want to buy.

Brazilian money

Local fruits

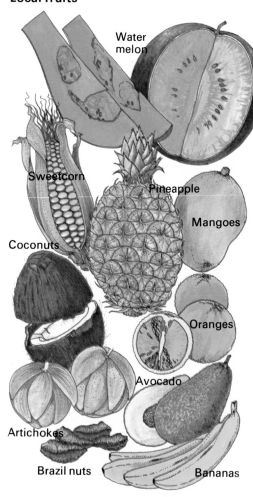

Water melon

Sweetcorn

Pineapple

Coconuts

Mangoes

Oranges

Avocado

Artichokes

Brazil nuts

Bananas

▲ Brazilians eat more fruit per person than in any other country in the world.

▼ Nowadays all the towns and cities have their supermarkets which are little different from those in other parts of the world. However, they only cater for a minority. Most Brazilians still buy their goods in smaller shops.

▶ City dwellers seldom have to bother about finding what they want to buy. Apart from the large stores, whole streets are given over to a jumble of shops, often family-owned, which all compete to sell the customer exactly what he wants.

▲ Shopping can still be an adventure in Brazil. Frequently, listed prices are only a rough guideline and the actual price is reached by mutual agreement. Brazilians are a naturally excitable people and derive great enjoyment from haggling, although there may be occasions when the negotiations become heated.

◀ Noisy, crowded and picturesque, the street markets can be found everywhere from the smallest villages to the largest cities. Prices are generally lower than in the shops and they provide a useful outlet for small producers who would have no other way of selling what they grow and make. Many of them do not have a stall. They simply lay out their produce on the ground.

15

Rio – the old capital

▶ One of the best ways to admire Rio de Janeiro is from the mountains on the landward side of the city, as this panoramic view towards the Sugar Loaf illustrates. Squeezed between the mountains and the sea, Rio is fast running out of room for expansion and in some places is no more than a few streets wide.

Road tunnels have had to be bored through outcrops of rock to connect various parts of the city and several hills have been completely flattened, the surplus soil being used to reclaim part of Guanabara Bay.

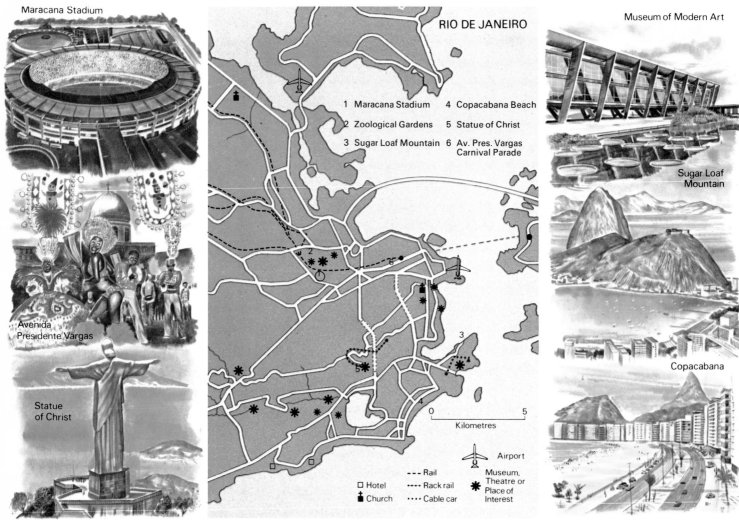

Maracana Stadium

Avenida Presidente Vargas

Statue of Christ

RIO DE JANEIRO

1 Maracana Stadium   4 Copacabana Beach

2 Zoological Gardens   5 Statue of Christ

3 Sugar Loaf Mountain   6 Av. Pres. Vargas Carnival Parade

0   5
Kilometres

✈ Airport

□ Hotel   --- Rail   ✈ Museum, Theatre or Place of Interest

⛪ Church   ···· Rack rail

    ···· Cable car

Museum of Modern Art

Sugar Loaf Mountain

Copacabana

A spectacular city

"God created the most beautiful scenery in the world in which the mountains, the sea and the white sands of the beaches harmonize in a site of rare natural beauty. Within this scenic, dream-like setting man built a truly marvellous city."

So say the citizens of Rio de Janeiro and most foreign visitors would agree with them. Although Brasilia is now the seat of government and Sao Paulo is the country's largest city, Rio still holds a very special place in the hearts of Brazilians. With its important artistic, literary and scientific institutions, it remains Brazil's cultural capital and is the major attraction for foreign tourists. The citizens of Rio, the *Cariocas*, are famed for their wit and volubility, their leisurely approach to life and their ability to enjoy themselves.

Copacabana, Corcovado and the Sugar Loaf

Despite its rich history as capital of the colony, empire and republic, Rio is most famous for its scenic beauties. It is the natural setting which has the main appeal for visitors. Copacabana and Ipanema beaches are internationally renowned for their sun-drenched sands and also for one of the world's biggest works of art, the gigantic pavement mosaic extending along the Avenida Atlantica beside the beach.

Overlooking Copacabana is Corcovado, 704 metres high and crowned by the imposing statue of Christ the Redeemer which is floodlit at night. Rising out of the cloud, it seems that Christ is protecting the city below. Other favourite tourist spots include the Sugar Loaf, with its cable railway, and the magnificent Botanical Gardens.

However, Rio is far more than a delight for tourists. It is also a major commercial and financial centre and it ranks behind Sao Paulo as Brazil's second industrial city. Noise, overcrowding, pollution and traffic congestion are all part of daily life in Rio and more than one million *Cariocas* live in the *favelas*, or slums.

Nevertheless, few other cities can claim such a striking blend of natural beauty and contemporary architecture. With $4\frac{1}{2}$ million citizens, Rio is the second largest city in Brazil.

▲ Life for the poor can be extremely hard. Electricity, running water and proper sewerage do not exist and the houses may be little more than shacks. Every city has its slums, called *favelas*, and so far the government has found no way to eradicate them. Here, the *favelas* of Rio are a sorry contrast to the wealth of the city centre and the dwellings are merely flimsy huts, built from odd scraps and rubbish. They are inhabited by the thousands of people who are drawn to the city from the rural areas in search of work.

▲ There can be few more pleasant places to relax and enjoy a drink or meal than in one of the pavement cafés overlooking the sea. You need never be alone there either. While you sit at your table, shoe-shine boys will offer to clean your footwear, beggars will ask for alms and ticket touts will try to interest you in the lottery. You might even be offered the opportunity to buy semi-precious stones smuggled from the interior.

▶ Rio de Janeiro prides itself on being the most sophisticated and cosmopolitan of all Brazilian cities, an attitude which is hotly contested by the citizens of Sao Paulo. For the *Cariocas* (inhabitants of Rio) everywhere else in Brazil is provincial but this does not stop them from being very hospitable to visitors. In the summer months Rio's streets are less crowded. People try to avoid the heat by going to resorts in the hills.

Sun, sand and samba

▼ The federal and state lotteries with their large cash prizes are an important weekly event. Some people will spend their last *cruzeiro* to buy the ticket of their choice. Football pools have also become popular recently.

The praia

Copacabana is not the only beach in Brazil – there are another 6500 kilometres of sand. Much of the population lives on or near the coast and the *praia*, or beach, is easily the most popular place for Brazilians to spend their leisure. In many cities the beach is a focus of social life and Brazilians who do not live near the sea head for the beach at every opportunity.

The beaches are for everybody, rich and poor, old and young. Children do homework there, businessmen close important deals and full-scale football and volleyball tournaments are organized on the sands.

The beaches are also busy commercial centres. Vendors roam the sands selling Coca-cola, beer, green coconuts, fruit, sunglasses, ices, kites and swimming costumes. They enable entire families to spend their days in the sun without ever moving from the beach.

Getting together

Although television is increasingly popular, the hot climate makes city apartments uncomfortable and most leisure activities take place away from the home. Sports events of all descriptions attract huge crowds and the pavement cafes are always busy.

For the poor, social life is centred on the street and city pavements are crowded night and day. Everybody who can afford it is a member of a private club. These all serve food and drink and most of them have at least one swimming pool.

Brazilians are famous for their love of singing and dancing and samba is the national music. During Carnival time the samba beat seems to be everywhere and the streets become huge, outdoor dance floors. Singers like Roberto Carlos, Caetano Velloso and Roberto Gil have a wide following throughout the country.

▼ Open-air paper and magazine stalls can be found in all the towns, often with the newspapers hung out on lines like washing. Glossy, illustrated magazines are widely read, as are the many periodicals which deal exclusively with sport.

▼ For some people fishing is nothing more than a pleasant means of relaxation. For many others along the coast it is a matter of economic necessity. The country's immense coastline and teeming rivers provide unlimited fishing, even for amateurs.

▲ Pavement bars and cafés do not simply offer a brief respite from the sun. They are often social centres and, as the Brazilians are a talkative people, discussions tend to be lively. *Cachaca*, the national drink, is made from fermented cane alcohol.

▼ Weekends are not the only times that Brazilian beaches are crowded. Many people enjoy a swim before work and the beach is frequently a meeting place in the evenings. At the height of summer, sunshades are a necessary protection.

Education

▼ In such a huge country, with many people living in remote rural areas, it is difficult to provide schools for everybody, but the building of new schools has been given government priority. Although it will be several years before every Brazilian child is guaranteed a place at school, between 1963 and 1974 the numbers of pupils at primary schools increased from 11 to 20 million.

A privilege, not a right

Brazilian education is still suffering from the legacy of the past. For many years it was sadly neglected and illiteracy is still one of the major problems facing the country. The first university was not established until 1920 and although a law was passed at the end of the 19th century providing free primary education for all, it was never properly implemented before 1930.

Despite efforts to improve standards since then, there are almost 20 million illiterate people in Brazil today. In more remote areas there may be no schools at all. Even in the cities there are some children who never attend school, while others only have a half-time education. It is not unusual for city schools to operate in shifts, with two or three batches of pupils being taught in the same building each day.

Although a national campaign for literacy commenced in 1970, teaching methods are often old-fashioned, facilities may be inadequate and there is an acute shortage of properly trained teachers.

Schools and universities

The education system provides for 8 years of compulsory schooling, starting when children are 7, followed by a 3-year pre-university course. In practice, more than half the pupils who attend public primary schools only have 4 years education since there are not enough public secondary places for everybody.

A high proportion of secondary schools are private and entrance to most of them, whether public or private, is by examination. An increasing number of students are going to universities and technical colleges but here too there is a shortage of places.

A growing population

Although great advances have been made in recent years, the population is growing faster than the state can provide schools and teachers. An important part of the government's programme has been to improve the technical and agricultural colleges which have long been one of the weakest links in the educational chain.

As yet, Brazil has no great scientific tradition, but research centres into tropical agriculture have acquired a reputation which extends far beyond the borders of Brazil.

The Brazilian school system

Nursery School (Private) 4–6 years

Primary School (Private or Public) 7–11 years

Secondary School (Mainly Public) 12–15 years

Ginásio (Usually Private) 12–15 years

Secondary School (Pre-university course mainly public) 16–18 years

Colégio (Usually Private) 16–18 years

University (Private and Public) 18+

Technical and Agricultural Colleges

Other Higher Education 18+

Post Graduate Courses

▲ The best Brazilian schools are very good indeed. Much of the teaching is by rote and pupils often have to provide their own schoolbooks. More and more girls are now going to university.

▶ In the fifty or so years since the first university was founded, standards have improved beyond recognition. Today there are nearly sixty seats of higher education in Brazil with a total enrolment of more than one million students.

▼ A Caraja Indian mission school in the interior. Educational opportunities vary tremendously in different parts of the country and many of the best schools are private. In cities like Sao Paulo and Rio nearly all children attend primary school but the same is not always true in the interior. Classes are usually small, and the teaching is basic.

▼ MOBRAL, the Brazilian Literacy Movement, is an educational system for adults, making use of volunteer teachers. Great progress has already been made and by 1980 it is hoped that all people under 35 will be literate. Many other adults improve their education by attending night school.

▼ Over half the population of Brazil is under 20, which means that a large number of new schools have to be built each year simply to keep pace with population growth. This is why so many private schools and colleges are needed to supplement the public school system.

A country of churches

▶ Salvador was the first capital of Brazil and, thanks to a federal commission, it is one city where the old churches have been preserved. The beautiful church of Sao Francisco Convent is the best known. All the interior woodwork was hand carved and then covered with gold. The money for this was provided by the local sugar barons.

▲ When the Portuguese established a settlement, the church was usually one of the first buildings erected, and many small Brazilian towns are still dominated by these old colonial churches. In the cities, however, many fine churches have been destroyed in the name of progress.

The largest Catholic country

Nine out of every ten Brazilians are Roman Catholics, making Brazil the largest Catholic country in the world. Missionaries accompanied the original settlers and, throughout its history, the Church has played a major part in the unification of the country.

All over Brazil there are beautiful and ornate churches, ranging from the baroque splendour of Salvador's Sao Francisco to the ultra-modern cathedral at Brasilia.

Priests and nuns are an everyday sight in the streets and, apart from being one of the largest landowners, the Church also plays an important role in education and medicine. Going to church is usually a regular part of weekly routine.

In recent years the Church has taken an increasing interest in secular affairs. On occasions, this has brought it into conflict with the government who have accused the Church of interference in areas outside its proper jurisdiction. This has been especially so in the north-east. Here, under the leadership of Dom Helder Camara, Archbishop of Recife, churchmen have led the attack on poverty, malnutrition and illiteracy.

Saints and festivals

A quick glance at a map shows that it is not only Brazilian children who are christened with saints' names. Sao Paulo and Sao Luis are only two of the cities to be named after saints while many others, such as Natal, also have place-names with a religious origin. Consequently, it is hardly surprising that church festivals should play such an important part in Brazilian life with nearly every village, town and city celebrating its own special day.

One of the greatest national festivals is on June 23rd, the Dia de Sao Joao. There are processions in the street, often in costume, and at night there are bonfires and fireworks. Good Friday is another of the most important feast days. It is celebrated with masses, and candlelit processions wind through the streets. In some small towns the entire population may join in.

Most Brazilians wear some kind of religious medallion or ornament. Nossa Senhora da Aparecida, Brazil's patron saint, features on many of them. All taxi, lorry and bus drivers have pictures of St Christopher stuck to their dashboards to bring them good luck on the roads.

▶ The statue of Christ the Redeemer on the summit of Corcovado in Rio de Janeiro is a striking indication of Brazilian Catholicism. Standing 30 metres high, the monument is one of the most spectacular sights in all of Latin America.

▲ The Nova Basilica is in honour of Brazil's patron saint, Nossa Senhora do Conceicao da Aparecida. The statue of the black Virgin Mary appeared to fishermen in the Paraiba river. When it floated upstream against the current, its miraculous powers were recognized and it was enshrined in its own cathedral.

▶ The black slaves brought their old beliefs from Africa with them and *macumba* remains a powerful influence. The religion has its own gods, such as Iemanja, Oxala and Exu, and it is particularly popular in the north-east. On New Year's Eve in Rio one million voodoo worshippers gather on Copacabana beach to pray to Iemanja.

▲ In large families one son frequently enters the church. There are many seminaries and monasteries in Brazil, especially in the north-east.

Football crazy!

▲ Football is not restricted to huge stadiums like Maracana Stadium in Rio, and lack of equipment is never an obstacle. If no boots are available, children are happy to play barefoot. Sometimes a bundle of rags may serve as a ball.

▼ Horse and trotting races draw thousands of spectators to each meeting and crowds are especially large in Rio and Sao Paulo. Fields are generally small but betting facilities at the tracks cater for the Brazilian love of gambling.

Almost another religion

Organized sport was not introduced into Brazil until this century but there are few other countries which are more sports conscious. Football is by far the most popular sport and Brazilians tend to take it very seriously indeed. After the national team's poor showing in the 1966 World Cup, the manager, who was held to be responsible for the failure, had to have armed police on guard outside his house for several weeks.

Normally, however, Brazilian teams are far more successful. Since the World Cup started, Brazil has reached the final stages on every occasion and has won the championship three times, in 1958, 1962 and 1970. This is a record which no other country can match.

Football heroes

Nearly every Brazilian supports one of the country's 20,000 football teams. Each state football association holds an annual cup competition and the winners go forward to contest the national trophy. Football is played everywhere, on the beach, in the streets, anywhere there is room to kick a ball around.

The players of leading clubs such as Flamengo, Santos and Fluminense receive the kind of adulation which is normally reserved for pop stars. Edson Arantes do Nascimento, better known as Pele, has been a national hero for the past decade and he scored over 1,000 goals before he left Brazilian football.

Rio's Maracana stadium is the shrine of Brazilian football, although there are other huge stadiums in Sao Paulo, Belo Horizonte and Porto Alegre. Maracana can hold 200,000 people, which makes it the largest football ground in the world. Crowds are noisy but generally good-tempered, and a feature of most matches is the drums, which play throughout the games.

Other sports as well

Although no other sport comes anywhere near to rivalling football for mass appeal, Brazilians enjoy most types of sport and tend to enjoy almost any form of competition. Television coverage has done much in recent years to enhance the popularity of several sports which hitherto had only a small following.

Horse racing is extremely popular throughout the country, not least because it is the only sport apart from football on which betting is allowed.

Brazilian sporting personalities

Nelson Pessoa

Garrincha

Maria Bueno

Pele

Ede Jofre

Emerson Fittipaldi

International success

Another sport which has attracted large crowds in the last few years has been motor racing. The international successes of Emerson Fittipaldi and Carlos Pace have done much to promote interest and Brazil now has its own Formula 1 racing car, the Copersucar. The Brazilian Grand Prix is held at Interlagos.

Other favourite sporting activities include athletics, boxing, swimming, lawn tennis, show jumping, wrestling, golf, volleyball and yachting. *Capoeira*, which is centred in the north-east, is one sport performed nowhere else apart from in Brazil. Originally a serious form of fighting, it is now a non-contact sport set against the background music of *capoeira's* own instrument, the *berimbau*. Although the tourists may see it as nothing more than an exotic kind of dance, contestants take it seriously and *capoeira* championships are regularly held.

▲ Like sport enthusiasts everywhere, Brazilians love nothing more than success and they have been exceptionally fortunate. Few other countries manage to defeat the national football team and players like Pele and Garrincha have become world famous. In lawn tennis the graceful Maria Bueno reigned supreme for several years while Jofre, the boxer, and Fittipaldi, the racing driver were both world champions. Nelson Pessoa is the leading Brazilian showjumper and has won many international tournaments.

▶ Part fight, part dance, *capoeira* is unique to Brazil. Its origins date from colonial days when masters used to punish slaves who were caught fighting. As a result the slaves disguised the actual fighting with music and dance. *Capoeira* is still popular in the north-east where it can either be a pure art form or a competitive sport.

The making of a nation

The first settlers

When Pedro Alvares Cabral landed on the north-eastern coast in 1500 and claimed the new territory for Portugal, he named it Terra da Vera Cruz – the Land of the True Cross. Within a few years it had changed to Brazil, a reference to *pau-brasil*, a red dye-wood which was much prized in Europe.

Development of the new colony was slow, largely because no precious metals were discovered. However, settlements were soon established at Sao Vicente and Olinda. The entire coast was marked off at 240-kilometre intervals to create the captaincies, hereditary land grants which became the administrative units.

Most of the early settlers were attracted to the north-east where huge plantations sprang up to cater for the Europeans' new-found taste for sugar. As the native Indians proved to be poor and unwilling workers, negro slaves were being brought from West Africa by the mid-16th century.

The Treaty of Tordesillas

If the Treaty of Tordesillas had been strictly adhered to, only the north-east of Brazil would have come under Portuguese rule. Fortunately the demarcation line was very vague and the Portuguese settlers chose to interpret the treaty to their own advantage. As a result, half of South America was to come under their control.

The bandeirantes

The *bandeirantes*, or flag bearers, were the men who pushed the frontiers of Brazil westward. Most of them came from the captaincy of Sao Paulo and were of mixed Portuguese and Indian blood. Whole families, together with slaves and livestock, ventured far into the interior, searching for gold and more slaves. They were violent, rapacious and cruel, killing Indians and Jesuit missionaries alike, but without them there would have been no modern Brazil.

Some of their expeditions lasted for years, exploring much of Minas Gerais, Goias and the Mato Grosso. By the 18th century they had established many mining towns such as Ouro Preto. Today the *bandeirantes* are revered as the true founders of Brazil, and became the country's first folk heroes.

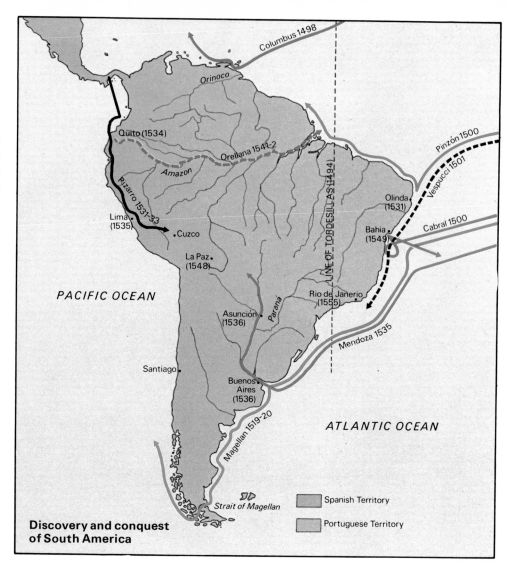

Discovery and conquest of South America

▲ The Treaty of Tordesillas was supposed to end disputes in the New World. A line was drawn 370 leagues from the Cape Verde Islands. All lands to the east of it were to belong to Portugal, all those to the west were to go to Spain. As the map shows, the terms of the treaty were never fulfilled. Thanks mainly to the *bandeirantes*, the areas under Portuguese control extended far beyond the line drawn at Tordesillas.

▶ Nobody knows who was the first European to set foot in Brazil but the country's effective discovery dates from 22 April, 1500 when Pedro Alvares Cabral claimed the land for Portugal. Supposedly on his way to India, Cabral sailed far to the west to avoid the calms off Africa and his landfall on the coast of Bahia was an accident. Cabral himself did not return to Brazil after he had claimed the new territory so he never knew how important his discovery was destined to be.

▶ The majority of Brazilian Indians were nomadic and the most advanced of them lived along the coast and near the mouth of the Amazon in semi-permanent villages. These were the Indians the early settlers first met. Although they were generally friendly, they were to prove unsuited for work on the plantations.

Europeans recorded this battle between two rival tribes during a 16th century voyage of discovery to Brazil.

▼ It was only in later years that travel in the jungle became so casual. The *bandeirantes* travelled in heavily-armed groups, often several hundred strong, and they seized what they wanted by force. This frequently brought them into conflict with the Jesuit missionaries who attempted to protect the Indians.

▼ It is estimated that there were about four million Indians in Brazil in 1500. They were scattered over the country in many distinct tribes and, as the shrunken heads suggest, some were both warlike and cannibalistic. Explorers first came into contact with the Tupi tribe, and used their language as a means of communication.

Pedro II and the Empire

▲ Scholarly and widely travelled, the Emperor Pedro II brought stability to Brazil at a time when it was badly needed.

▼ The Declaration of Ipiranga, September 7, 1822, marked Brazilian independence and Pedro I was acclaimed Emperor. He had ambitions in Portugal however, and returned there after his abdication in 1831.

The Empire

While Brazil remained a colony no great cities developed, wealth and property stayed in the hands of a privileged few and Portugal completely monopolized trade. Many Brazilians were resentful of Portuguese rule and there was widespread discontent, as was shown by the so-called Minas conspiracy, of 1789-1792. This was an ill-fated movement for independence under the leadership of Lieutenant Joaquim Jose da Silva Xavier, known as "Tiradentes" (Toothpuller) since he also practised dentistry.

The turning point came in 1807 when Napoleon invaded Portugal. This forced the Prince Regent, later to become King John VI, to move his entire court across the Atlantic to Rio de Janeiro. Many new settlers followed the royal family to Brazil, trade was freed and the colony was given equal status with Portugal.

Brazilian independence

The crisis came after King John had gone back to Portugal, leaving his son, Pedro, as regent. The Portuguese Cortes (parliament) wanted to return Brazil to its former status as a colony. When the Cortes ordered Dom Pedro to return to Portugal he refused. Backed by most Brazilians, he declared Brazilian independence on September 7, 1822. A few months later he was crowned as Brazil's first Emperor.

It was during the 49-year rule of his son,

Pedro II, that Brazil enjoyed one of its most progressive and prosperous eras. Pedro II was a democratic ruler who took his duties seriously and he was popular with the ordinary people. It was a period of expansion. The population increased threefold, roads and railways were introduced and much was done to improve the machinery of government. It was under Pedro II that Brazil first learned how to govern itself.

Slave emancipation

The major social and economic problem of Pedro II's reign was that of slavery. Although the Emperor freed his own slaves as early as 1840, emancipation was far more difficult to achieve in the country as a whole. The Brazilian economy depended almost entirely on agriculture and the great sugar, coffee and cotton plantations which provided the bulk of Brazil's wealth all relied on slave labour.

Pedro II found himself caught in the middle between those who wanted abolition and the plantation owners who were violently opposed to the notion of losing their cheap labour force. After a great deal of controversy and a process of gradual emancipation, slavery was finally abolished in 1888. It cost the Emperor both the support of the landowners and his throne. Less than 18 months after slave emancipation Pedro II was forced to abdicate and a republic was proclaimed.

▲ Although slavery was the dominant issue in Brazilian politics under the Empire, slaves were treated far better than those elsewhere. The slaves in the picture are well dressed and full members of the household.

◄ The war against Paraguay, 1865-1870, when Brazil was allied with Argentina and Uruguay, proved to be an expensive victory. As a result of the war the railway and telegraph systems were expanded and there was a minor industrial boom.

▼ After the deposition of Pedro II a republican government was formed. Benjamin Constant provided inspiration for the revolt, which had the slogan of "order and progress", and it was led by Marshal da Fonseca who became President. Thanks largely to the Emperor's moderation, the transition led to little bloodshed.

The breakdown
of democracy

The breakdown of democracy

During the first years of the Republic Brazilian politics were dominated by the "coffee and milk" agreement. The states of Sao Paulo (with its coffee) and Minas Gerais (with its dairy herds) took it in turns to provide the President. In this way, they governed the country largely in their own interests. This led to a great deal of unrest among the people, and particularly among the military.

In 1930 the agreement broke down when the Paulistas (from Sao Paulo) attempted to nominate a second successive President. The Minas candidate, Getulio Vargas, thereupon joined forces with sympathizers from the army. After his defeat in the presidential elections Vargas accused his opponent of fraud and was swept into power by a popular revolt.

For a while Vargas retained the outward appearance of democracy, and submitted to the liberal constitution of 1934, although he resented its restrictions. A Communist-inspired revolt gave him the chance to declare a state of siege and in 1937 he seized absolute power by disbanding both houses of Congress. Yet another constitution was proclaimed and Vargas became dictator in everything but name. Many of his opponents were arrested, all political parties were suppressed and the press was severely censored.

Estado Novo

Nevertheless, the *Estado Novo* (the new State) brought some benefits to Brazil. Vargas himself remained popular with the masses and he attempted to bridge the huge gap between rich and poor. The antiquated educational system was overhauled and his encouragement of industry laid a sound foundation for Brazil's later prosperity.

Participation in World War II exposed Brazil to the democratic ideals of the Allies and in 1945 Vargas was deposed by a bloodless revolution. Even with the restoration of democracy he was still the dominant figure in domestic politics and in 1950 he won the presidential elections.

▲ Although Vargas was the Minas Gerais nominee in the presidential elections, he came from Rio Grande do Sul. The photograph shows volunteer helpers in his home state. 1930 was a troubled time for Brazil and Vargas's promises of electoral and political reform had wide appeal. The world depression had drastically reduced demand for coffee and this in turn had provoked a major financial crisis. There were frequent clashes between rival political groups and many Brazilians regarded Vargas as a national saviour.

▶ The Brazilian government declared war on Germany and Italy in August 1942. The Brazilian navy helped to patrol the South Atlantic in search of German submarines and the United States was allowed to use naval and air bases in Brazil. President Vargas is here seen inspecting members of the Brazilian Expeditionary Force on board a troop transport. The force went to Europe in July 1944, and distinguished itself in the Italian campaign.

Unfortunately for Vargas times had changed. He was unable to force his legislation through Congress and could not cope with the worsening economic crisis. Furthermore, his administration was riddled with corruption and when this was exposed Vargas was forced to resign in 1954. The next day he committed suicide and the Vargas era was at an end.

The military takes over

Despite rapid industrialization, the economic situation steadily deteriorated under Vargas's successors. Finally, under the radical but ineffective Joao Goulart, Brazil was on the verge of total economic collapse. In March 1964 the army stepped in to remove him from office and Marshal Humberto Castelo Branco replaced Goulart as President.

Since then the armed services have ruled Brazil. Under the regime there has been a vast improvement in the economy. Much of the corruption in government has been eradicated and the country has enjoyed a stable administration. However, this has only been achieved by strengthening the government and by the loss of certain civil liberties. Opponents of the regime claim that it is virtually a military dictatorship.

▲ Juscelino Kubitschek was President from 1956 until 1961. Convinced that Brazil was destined to be a great power, he undertook an ambitious programme of national development. Inter-regional highways were built, vast hydro-electric projects were commenced and industry was encouraged. His greatest achievement was the construction of Brasilia, but material progress under Kubitschek had a heavy price. Inflation reached fantastic proportions during his administration and the cost of living tripled. His expansion schemes required outside finance and the country's foreign debt more than doubled.

▲ Most Brazilians were enthusiastic about their country's participation in World War II. Salvaged heaps of scrap for the war effort are piled high on Rio's Avenida Rio Branco. Enthusiastic supporters of the war brandish a banner proclaiming "Democracy and Justice", a slogan which seems oddly at variance with Vargas's authoritarian regime. He was a dictator, and comparisons with the democracies who were Brazil's allies were to contribute to his overthrow.

▶ In 1960, the new capital of Brazil was inaugurated. Even as Brasilia was being built, a shanty-town sprang up on the outskirts of the city. Over 100,000 workers were involved in the construction and they lived in an area called Freetown. Today there is still the curious contrast of a beautiful modernistic city bordered by slums where people exist in the most primitive conditions.

31

The last great frontier

forest are completely uninhabited, apart from a few Indians. Except for the brief-lived rubber boom, the region has had little economic significance. The whole of Amazonia was virtually an economic vacuum but this is now changing dramatically.

The building of Brasilia provided the impetus for a determined drive into the interior. The Belem-Brasilia highway, the Transamazonica and other new roads are opening up the region.

The "lungs" of the earth

Many ecologists have expressed concern about these developments, however. The Amazon rain forest provides 40 per cent of the world's oxygen and they are worried about the effects of stripping the forest cover. Brazilians have no such doubts. Amazonia is their new frontier and each new inroad into the wilderness is seen as a step forward for Brazil.

◀ The dark waters of the Rio Negro meet the River Amazon. New roads are being built but the rivers still have an important role to play. They provide natural highways through the dense forest cover.

Wildlife of the Amazon

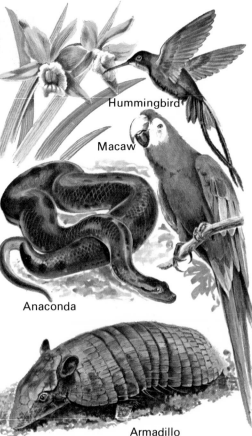

Hummingbird

Macaw

Anaconda

Armadillo

The king of rivers

The Nile may be longer but the Amazon is the largest river in the world. Nearly 6,500 kilometres long, the Amazon and its tributaries carry over 20 per cent of all the world's fresh water. Ocean-going ships can travel over 3218 kilometres upriver and at its mouth the Amazon is almost 320 kilometres wide.

The area drained by the river extends for over 6¼ million square kilometres and much of it is covered by forest. Every tenth tree on earth grows in the Amazon basin and plants of all kinds grow in profusion. Several thousand different species have been counted in one square kilometre.

Animals, birds and fishes

Wild life is also plentiful. Although the jaguar is becoming rare, land mammals include the capybara (the world's largest rodent), tapirs, wild pigs, water buffalo and the comical sloth. Many types of snake and insects live in the forest.

In the rivers piranhas and alligators may wait to trap the unwary and anacondas spend much time in the water. Two giant oddities are the pirarcu, the world's biggest freshwater fish, and the Amazon sea cow which may weigh almost a ton.

The trees themselves are equally well populated. Parrots, macaws, humming birds and many other exotic birds share the trees with the ever-present monkeys. Between them flutter the large, brightly coloured butterflies which are another feature of the Amazon.

A land of opportunity

Although the Amazon basin accounts for nearly half the total area of Brazil, less than 5 per cent of the population lives there, and most of them in the vicinity of Belem or Manaus. Hundreds of square kilometres of

▲ The floating docks at Manaus were specially designed to rise and fall with the 12-metre tide on the Rio Negro. They date back to the heady days when the city was the centre of the rubber boom.

▼ For thousands of years the only human inhabitants of the Amazon basin were scattered tribes of primitive Indians and the Amazon forest was the preserve of its animals. Despite man's subsequent encroachments, it remains the home of a fascinating variety of wildlife.

▲ Seen from the air, the Transamazonica is little more than a scratch on the vast forest carpet but for Brazilians it is a key to their nation's future.

▼ Many houses on the banks have to be built on stilts because of flooding. Even now, most of Amazonia's population is clustered beside the major rivers.

Tree frog

Howler monkey

Jaguar

Giant ant-eater

Vanishing tribes

Unwilling hosts

When the Portuguese first landed at the beginning of the 16th century they found no advanced Indian civilizations like those in Peru or Mexico. There were some settled tribes near the coast and along some of the rivers but most Indians were nomadic. Iron and bronze were unknown to them. They practised only the most primitive forms of agriculture and lived mainly by hunting and fishing.

At first, relations with the Portuguese were relatively peaceful but this soon changed when the colonists tried to employ the Indians as soldiers or slaves. Confronted by a civilization they did not understand, they either fought or fled into the forests of the Amazon and Mato Grosso.

Even in the interior they were not safe for long, despite the attempts of the Jesuit missionaries to defend them from the *bandeirantes*. Whole tribes died in battle or captivity, or from European diseases to which they had no resistance.

A dying race

Today there are less than 100,000 Indians left, although many millions of Brazilians have some Indian blood. Only a few small tribes still live the way their forefathers did before them. During this century great efforts have been made to protect the surviving Indians.

The soldier-explorer Marshal Rondon was an early advocate of making peace rather than extermination and today the Villas Boas brothers are famous throughout Brazil for their work among the tribes of the Xingu River. FUNAI, a government

▲ Every tribe had its own traditions and ceremonials. Nowadays few of them have managed to avoid contact with 20th-century civilization and the old ways are being changed. Tourism has come to the interior of Brazil and for some tribes ancient ceremonials and tribal costumes have become a means of earning money.

◀ The outline of the United States of America superimposed on a map of the Amazon basin. This gives some idea of the enormous area drained by the River Amazon and its tributaries.

▲ With the help of his brother, Orlando, Claudio Villas-Boas has devoted his adult life to protecting the Indians around the Xingu river from outside influences. He lives with them in the interior, only rarely returning to civilization.

agency, is officially responsible for preserving the Indians' culture and environment and over 80,000 Indians live on special reserves.

The Indian influence

Tribes like the Tupi, Tremembe, Nambiquara and Caraja might have vanished or be on the verge of extinction but the Indian influence remains. In early colonial days many Indian women interbred with the Portuguese settlers, and more than a third of Brazil's population has some Indian blood. In some regions, as among the *caboclos* of the north-eastern cattle area, the Indian strain is particularly evident.

The most influential tribe was the Tupi, which lived along the coast and was the first to come into contact with the Portuguese colonists. For more than 300 years Tupi was the second language of Brazil, rivalling Portuguese in importance, and hundreds of words of Indian derivation are still used.

Many place names are of Indian origin and even a city like Sao Paulo has streets with Indian names. Indian crops like manioc, yams, maize and sweet potatoes remain important. Throughout the interior primitive Indian folklore and agricultural practices are still significant.

▲ The rivers have always been a traditional source of food for the Indians. Some of them still make their canoes in the old way by hollowing or burning out a whole tree trunk. Apart from manioc, fish and meat from hunting they ate fruits, berries and nuts. Some tribes grew tubers and maize.

▼ Most Indian settlements, like this 'spoked-wheel' village near the Tocantins River, were only semi-permanent. There was often friction between neighbouring tribes and warfare was common. The most feared of all Indians were the Botocudo. These were exempted from early laws protecting tribes.

▲ The roots of the manioc, or cassava, were a staple food for many Indians and were used for flour, bread and alcoholic drinks. The root is poisonous and had to be grated, squeezed and heated before it was safe to eat. It is unique in that the roots remain fresh indefinitely so long as they are left in the ground and manioc is still widely grown. Tapioca is made from it.

Brasilia – a dream come true

An old idea

In 1883 a Brazilian monk called Dom Bosco had a prophetic dream. In his dream, he was travelling by train when he witnessed the murder of two monks by Indians. After he woke he described the spot exactly and predicted that within two generations the promised land would appear there. Eighty years later the place he saw in his dream became the site of Brasilia and Dom Bosco has a chapel named after him in the city.

However, the origins of Brasilia date back much further. The Marquis de Pombal first suggested an interior capital before the seat of government had been moved from Salvador to Rio, and it was an idea which was discussed again and again in the years which followed. The name Brasilia and its approximate site had been suggested by the mid-19th century and in 1891 the idea of a new capital was embodied in the constitution.

Kubitschek and the creation of Brasilia

It was left to Juscelino Kubitschek to convert the dream into reality. When he became President in 1956 he wanted to do something which would always be remembered, and Brasilia was his answer. Despite the country's economic problems, he pressed the work forward so vigorously that the new capital was officially inaugurated in 1960, although much of the construction was still unfinished.

Kubitschek's ambitions were not the only reason for the building of Brasilia. It was felt that if the capital were moved inland from the coast, impetus would be given to the development of the sparsely populated and economically backward interior. Brasilia was to be the symbol of a reborn, united nation and so far it has more than lived up to Kubitschek's hopes.

▲ The blocks of flats, which are separated from the roads by wide expanses of grass lawns, were designed as self-contained communities. Each block has its own shops and schools. The population of Brasilia has increased rapidly. Well over half a million people now live in the Federal District.

▼ Partially enclosed by a huge, man-made lake, Brasilia was laid out in the shape of an aeroplane. The fuselage is formed by a wide boulevard, flanked by various public buildings and leading up to Three Powers Square. The wings extending on either side are made up of the residential and shopping areas.

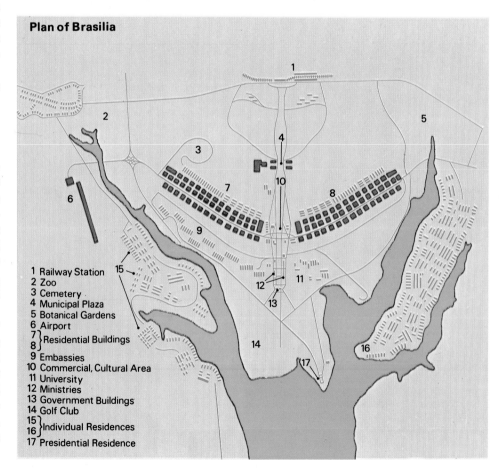

Plan of Brasilia

1 Railway Station
2 Zoo
3 Cemetery
4 Municipal Plaza
5 Botanical Gardens
6 Airport
7 } Residential Buildings
8 }
9 Embassies
10 Commercial, Cultural Area
11 University
12 Ministries
13 Government Buildings
14 Golf Club
15 } Individual Residences
16 }
17 Presidential Residence

A city of the future

Thousands of people were involved in the construction of Brasilia but Lucio Costa and Oscar Niemeyer must take most credit for making the city unique. Costa's overall city plan was one of striking simplicity. He envisaged Brasilia as a park city and everywhere he tried to blend nature with the needs of a modern city by making full use of open spaces and planned landscapes. One unusual feature was that pedestrians were kept completely separate from motorists and the road system was planned without intersections or traffic lights.

At first there was some reluctance among government officials to leave the comforts of Rio, but this was soon overcome and the city has grown rapidly since its inauguration. It has become the focus of an extensive road network, and has spurred economic growth in the area surrounding it.

Architecturally, Brasilia lives up to its claim of being a city of the 21st century. It is a capital like no other. Niemeyer's designs for the Congress buildings, the cathedral, the Presidential Palaces and the Ministry of Foreign Affairs are among the most beautiful examples of modern architecture to be found anywhere. What was a wilderness in 1957 has become the site of a spectacular city which symbolizes Brazilian determination to unite the underdeveloped interior and the cities on the coast.

▲ Seen across a shallow ornamental lake, the twin towers of Congress soar into the air. They house the offices of the senators and deputies. The bowls on either side of the towers are the House of Deputies and the Senate chamber. The fleecy cloud formations beyond are a typical feature of Brasilia.

◀ Brasilia is far more than the seat of government and an architectural showpiece. When the ministries moved there from Rio so did most of the important financial institutions such as the Central Bank and the Bank of Brazil. Since its inauguration the city has become the commercial centre for a large area of the interior and many large national companies now have their headquarters there.

Eating the Brazilian way

A little bit of everything

Like so much else, Brazilian eating habits are essentially regional and, with the possible exception of *feijoada*, there is no national dish. Amazonia, the north-east and the south all have their distinctive dishes, many of them unique to a particular region.

However, there is one thing all Brazilians do have in common – they are big eaters. They also enjoy variety. It is not unusual for meat and fish to be served on the same plate, along with rice, vegetables, salad and anything else which takes the fancy. So long as the food tastes good, Brazilians don't mind mixing it.

Consequently, there is no normal daily menu, except for the very poor. Breakfast, with its milky coffee and buttered bread or rolls, is standard all over the country. For other meals anything goes, according to individual preference. In general, though, Brazilians eat a lot of meat and fish and relatively few vegetables apart from rice. One standard vegetable which would be considered a delicacy anywhere else is heart of palm. Brazilians also eat more fruit per head than in any other country.

Restaurants

For those who can afford it, eating out is a regular family activity and the many types of cooking reflect the Brazilians' liking for variety. Most city restaurants have an international flavour. Portuguese, Italian, French, German, Hungarian and Japanese dishes are all popular, with Chinese restaurants an especial favourite. Other restaurants concentrate on regional foods and there are plenty of cheaper eating places for those who need them.

A colourful tradition

Of all the regional dishes, those from Bahia are the most famous. They originated in colonial days when the slave women had to use every available scrap of food. *Abara, vatapa, caruru* and *serapatel* are among the best known and most of them are cooked in coconut milk or palm oil.

Churrasco from Rio Grande do Sul is another popular dish. Pieces of beef or some other meat are skewered on a metal sword and cooked over hot coals or charcoal. It is usually served with salad and tomato and onion sauce.

▼Indian, African, Portuguese and other European influences have all affected Brazilian cuisine and each region has its own specialities. The dishes below are from the north-east where the African influence was at its strongest.

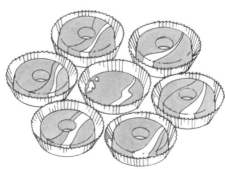

▲Coconut in some form or other is an ingredient in most Bahian cooking. The coconut cup cakes above *(quindins de yaya)* are a typical delicacy.

▲ *Vatapa* is one of the most famous Bahian dishes. The principal ingredients are fish, shrimps, rice flour, ginger, dendé oil and coconut milk served over white rice.

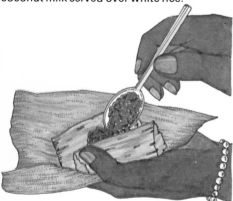

▲ *Abara* is another north-eastern meal. A mixture of prawns and black-eyed peas or beans is spiced with pepper and dendé oil. After cooking it is wrapped in banana leaves.

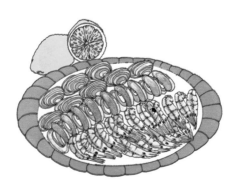

▲ Meat was hard to come by for the slaves. Instead the women made full use of local seafood. Prawns, lobster and other kinds of shellfish are popular throughout Brazil.

Feijoada – the national dish

Feijoada is more of an institution than a national dish and Saturday lunchtime is when it is usually eaten. Rice and black beans are the staple diet of the poor and, in its simplest form, *feijoada* was a poor man's meal. Now it is a weekly treat for just about everybody.

Ingredients

3lb smoked ox tongue; 1lb pork spare-ribs; $\frac{1}{2}$lb spiced pork sausages; $\frac{1}{2}$lb fresh pork sausages; $1\frac{1}{2}$lbs dried black beans; 1lb chuck beef; 1 pig's trotter; 4oz lean bacon; $\frac{1}{2}$lb smoked bacon; 6oz chopped onions; 1oz lard; 3 chopped tomatoes; 2 finely chopped tabasco peppers; clove of garlic; seasoning.

Method

Soak tongue and spare ribs overnight. Then cover tongue with water and simmer for 3–4 hours. Cover spare ribs, pig's trotter, spiced and fresh sausage with water. Bring to the boil, then simmer for $\frac{1}{4}$ hour and set aside.

Boil beans in 5 pints water for 2 minutes, then leave to soak for 1 hour. Add bacon, pig's trotter and spare ribs. Bring to the boil, then reduce heat, cover and simmer for 1 hour. Use more boiling water if beans get too dry.

Add chuck beef and continue cooking for 1 hour. Add spiced and fresh sausage

▲ Although Brazilian food is varied and often delicious, many city restaurants serve an international cuisine. When Brazilians go out for a meal they usually like to eat something different from what they have at home.

▶ For those who have no time to enjoy a restaurant meal there is no need to go hungry. In busy sections of the towns and cities roadside vendors sell everything from soup to full meals. Kebabs are a favourite.

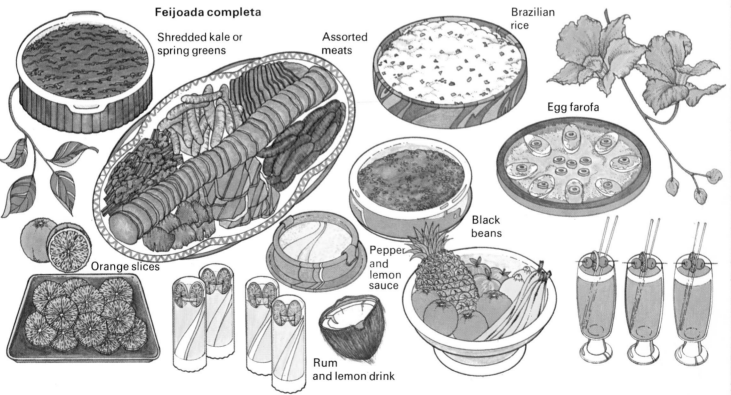

Feijoada completa

Shredded kale or spring greens

Assorted meats

Brazilian rice

Egg farofa

Orange slices

Black beans

Pepper and lemon sauce

Rum and lemon drink

and smoked bacon and cook for ½ hour. Skim fat, add tongue. Remove from heat.

Melt lard in frying pan. Cook onions and garlic until onions are translucent. Stir in tomatoes, tabasco peppers, and seasoning. Simmer for 5 minutes. Drain

¾ of beans from saucepan and add to frying pan. Mash in thoroughly, adding ¾ pint of bean liquid. Simmer sauce until thick (about ¼ hour). Put sauce into pan with beans and meats. Keep at low heat for 20 minutes. Assemble as in picture.

Pepper and lemon sauce
Put 4 chopped tabasco peppers, 6 tbs. finely chopped onions, 6 tbs. lemon juice and crushed garlic in small bowl. Marinate for 1 hour.

Serve *feijoada* over rice, with side dishes.

Custom and superstition

▲ Many superstitious people invariably wear a *figa*, a good luck charm in the shape of a clenched fist with the thumb sticking up between the first and second fingers. If it is to be effective in warding off evil it must be a gift — it is no good buying one for yourself.

▲ Most towns have a particular street or streets closed to traffic in the evening. Groups of young women or young men parade up and down, allowing members of the opposite sex an opportunity to admire their charms and flirt with them.

▲ *Galleto al primo canto* is a favourite dish in Rio Grande do Sul. It is made using a young cockerel which has just crowed for the very first time. The unfortunate rooster is then cut into pieces, placed on a spit and basted in white wine and oil.

▲ *Cachaca*, which is fermented cane alcohol, is Brazil's national drink and is sometimes referred to as the whisky of the poor. Some people always spit the first mouthful of *cachaca* on the floor to prevent evil spirits entering their body.

Carnival

The annual Carnival in Rio has been called the greatest show on earth and it is celebrated with equal fervour throughout the length and breadth of Brazil. For four days and five nights every year all commercial life stops. All shops and businesses close and the entire population gives itself over to pleasure. Traffic grinds to a halt in the city centres and the streets are packed with singing and dancing people, many of whom do not sleep at all for the duration of Carnival.

Lavish costume balls are held in the towns and cities but the street parades, involving thousands of people, are the real highlight. Originally Carnival was a church festival, but it has gradually changed and now it is a festival of the people.

Although it does not take place until February or March, the samba bands start practising months beforehand and some of the poorer people will go hungry so they can afford the ornate costumes they will wear in the parades. Carnival in Rio has become so famous that it attracts visitors from all over the world.

Legend and folklore

Brazil has a wealth of folklore. Ghosts, witches and strange beasts are talked about all over the country and there are spells to ensure everything from the faithfulness of a husband to an abundant harvest. The majority of these folk-tales have African origins but the Indians have their superstitions as well and some of the demons who inhabit the Amazon forests are terrifying characters. Two of the most fearsome are *Caruara*, who preys on pregnant women, and the *Capelobo*, who has an anteater's head on a human body and kills lone travellers.

One of the most popular figures is Saci-Perere. Smoking a pipe and hopping around on one leg, he is always involved in some kind of mischief and he delights in playing practical jokes. Children often make Saci-Perere a scapegoat for their own misdeeds.

The spirits of the dead

A date to beware of is November 2 when the spirits of the dead are supposed to return to earth, many of them with wrongs to avenge. Superstitious Brazilians avoid those places where people are known to have died for this is where the ghosts first return. On the other hand, the Dia de Sao Joao is an auspicious day for spinsters to find themselves a husband.

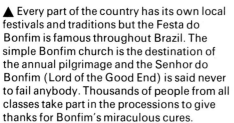

▲ Every part of the country has its own local festivals and traditions but the Festa do Bonfim is famous throughout Brazil. The simple Bonfim church is the destination of the annual pilgrimage and the Senhor do Bonfim (Lord of the Good End) is said never to fail anybody. Thousands of people from all classes take part in the processions to give thanks for Bonfim's miraculous cures.

▶ Carnival began as a simple celebration of Shrove Tuesday. Gradually, over the years, it has been transformed into the spectacle it has become today, a festival which brings the commercial life of the nation to a dead halt. In Rio there are samba clubs, usually associated with a particular neighbourhood and they spend the whole year preparing their song and dance routines for the street parades. Each year Carnival has a general theme and prizes are awarded for the best displays.

Getting about in Brazil

A major problem

It is no coincidence that Brazil has so many distinct regions, for throughout its history many areas have lacked any means of communication with the rest of the country. Indeed, inadequate road and rail facilities have long held back the economic development of Brazil as a whole, making it impossible to exploit Brazil's resources to the full. Any improvements were usually at regional rather than national level.

Over the last 20 years an attempt has been made to put matters right, with the federal government assuming responsibility for overall co-ordination. However, even today there are some parts of Brazil which are connected to the rest of the country solely by river or air.

Although the first railway was built as early as 1854, there are still only 30,000 kilometres of track and away from the big cities, rail services are restricted. There are few links between the various lines, most rolling stock is old and there are three different gauges.

This means that trucks and lorries have to carry many essential goods which would be better transported by rail. The road system too is inadequate. Despite major expansion of the road network since 1956, especially away from the coast, most of the roads are unpaved away from the urban areas and may become impassable in bad weather.

River transport

River transport is important along the Amazon, Jacui and Sao Francisco, but few navigable rivers flow near the main population centres. For some regions, coastal shipping is the only viable means of transport and internal air routes connect most of the country.

The government is well aware of the problem and is making strenuous efforts to improve communications. New highways like the Transamazonica are a sign of Brazil's determination to build a transport system worthy of such a great nation.

▲ VARIG is Brazil's major international airline but Cruzeiro do Sul, VASP and Transbrasil are also important. Distances are so great that aeroplanes are often the only practicable means of transport and regular air taxis fly between the biggest cities. People who can afford it may prefer not to rely on the airlines, and maintain their own private aircraft instead.

◀ Many Brazilians still travel to market by traditional means of transport. Quite apart from their cost, cars are not always a practical proposition. Most of the roads in the interior are unpaved and after heavy rain they may become unfit for motor vehicles.

▼ The rush hour in Brazilian cities can produce traffic jams as bad as anywhere in the world. This is particularly the case in Rio and Sao Paulo and many motorists consider a loud horn to be essential.

▲ Cars are still expensive in Brazil but bus fares are cheap and most city buses are crowded. Now that so many new roads have been built, long-distance buses are becoming increasingly important. It is now possible to travel the length of Brazil by coach.

▼ In the Amazon basin the river steamer remains a popular means of transport. It is a leisurely way to travel, with stops being made at every riverside village. As the hammocks suggest, the longer journeys may last for several days.

▼ Although there are extensive modern rail networks around the major urban centres, there are only 30,000 kilometres of track in the entire country. Most of these lines are near the coast.

The Brazilian character

A tolerant people

Brazilians are very different from their South American neighbours and this is not simply because they speak Portuguese instead of Spanish. Elsewhere on the continent revolutions are bloody affairs but this has rarely happened in Brazil. Indeed, tolerance is the keynote to the Brazilian character and they are seldom dogmatic about anything – unless they are discussing the respective merits of their favourite football teams!

Politics and politicians are regarded with more cynicism than passion and discrimination based on race or colour is virtually unknown. Brazilians are so easygoing it almost becomes a fault. They tend to accept life as they find it and derive as much pleasure as possible from what they do.

A leisurely approach

Paradoxically, Brazilians are also very emotional and it is no disgrace for them to put their feelings on public display. The *abraco*, the embrace on meeting a friend, is common to both sexes. Sympathy is readily offered to those who need it and a Brazilian can always be relied on to give help and advice to a friend. Most people like to air their views and offer their opinions on various topics. The resulting discussions may be heated, but are hardly ever bad-tempered. Possibly the strongest emotion of all is the love of family.

At times the Brazilian approach to life seems too leisurely. Punctuality is definitely not one of their virtues and, if anything interesting should happen in the street, a Brazilian always has time to watch developments before proceeding about his business. The national motto often appears to be "Never do today what can be put off until tomorrow".

Machismo and Brazilian men

Brazilian men take their masculinity very seriously and appearances have to be maintained at all costs. It is not enough to be male, other people must be made aware of virility. This can lead to much self-conscious posturing, an unusual characteristic to find among a people normally so quick to poke fun at the absurd. Men are especially possessive in their attitudes towards their wives and girlfriends.

Getting round the problem

Another feature of the Brazilian way of life is the *jeito*, the belief that there is a way round every problem. Bribery is not nearly so widespread as it used to be but a few *cruzeiros* wisely invested are still the answer to many difficulties. Usually the *jeito* is the knack of obtaining faster and better service or of pulling the strings which will help you to jump ahead of the rest of the queue.

▲ Brazilians take great pride in their appearance and a pair of well polished shoes is essential. There are always plenty of shoe-shine boys eager to do the work, either in special shops or out on the streets.

▶ Rushing around is not part of the national character. Brazilians believe in taking life at an easy pace and they enjoy a sociable chat with their friends. The people of Brazil are both talkative and friendly and there is usually plenty of gossip to exchange when a group of housewives get together.

► The colour of a person's skin has little significance in Brazil and there are very few people without some Indian or Negro blood. A person's character is far more important than his appearance and there is relatively little discrimination. Brazil comes closer than any other nation to having a truly multi-racial society.

▲ Children make up nearly half of the country's population and Brazilians are doting parents. Although they always expect their children to pay a proper respect, parents are generally both indulgent and affectionate.

▼ Parties are often spontaneous and almost invariably boisterous. If the music is good and there is plenty to eat and drink the gathering is a guaranteed success. Brazilians believe in enjoying themselves and on national holidays and feast days whole villages may become involved. Many parties are held out of doors.

▲ Life is not always safe on the roads. Brazilians tend to be fast, flamboyant drivers, often paying little attention to traffic regulations, and the rule of the road is every man for himself. Crossing a busy city street can be an adventure.

The lively arts

▲ Sao Paulo rivals Rio as a cultural centre and the Museum of Modern Art is only one of the city's fine museums. A famous exhibition of modern art, the Bienal, is held in Sao Paulo every other year.

▶ Emiliano di Cavalcanti is Brazil's most famous living artist. A friend of Picasso, he shocked the Brazilian art world when he burst onto the scene in the 1920's. *Cinco mocas de Guaratingueta* is typical of his work.

The problem of communication

Although there were few countries where more respect was shown for the arts, Brazilian painting, music and literature made little international impact until the 20th century. In literature, the problem was, and is, mainly one of language. Portuguese was understood only in Portugal and Brazil itself so while there were many fine poets and novelists their works were only available to a limited public. The poetry of Goncalves Dias (1823-64) and the prose of Machado de Assis (1839-1908) and Euclides da Cunha (1866-1909) were not appreciated outside Brazil until long after their deaths.

Regional influences

In painting, sculpture and music the artists had a geographical problem to overcome. Nearly all the work was regional, reflecting the country's varied racial and cultural origins, and to a certain extent this remains true today. Different parts of Brazil still lack easy means of communication with one another and artists who are popular in Recife may be virtually unknown in Rio.

It was only in the 1920's that a truly national style began to emerge. This was most strikingly apparent in architecture. The government encouraged new ideas and the buildings of men like Oscar Niemeyer, Lucio Costa and Jorge Moriera have been admired all over the world.

This new sense of national identity was shown in other art forms as well. Candido Portinari and Emiliano di Cavalcanti in painting, Heitor Villa-Lobos in music and Jorge Amado in literature merely represent the peaks of a great artistic awakening in Brazil.

The Little Cripple

The most remarkable figure in Brazilian art was Antonio Francisco Lisboa (1730-1814), better known as 'O Aleijadinho' (the Little Cripple). The son of a Negro slave and a Portuguese stonemason, Aleijadinho contracted a terrible disease while he was still young but for 40 years he continued to work on the churches of Minas Gerais. When he could no longer walk, leather pads were tied to his knees and he crawled. When he lost the use of his hands, tools were strapped to the stumps of his arms. He worked until he was over 80 and many of his works survive today. Among his finest are the statues of the 12 Prophets at Congonhas do Campo and the church in Ouro Preto.

46

Local crafts

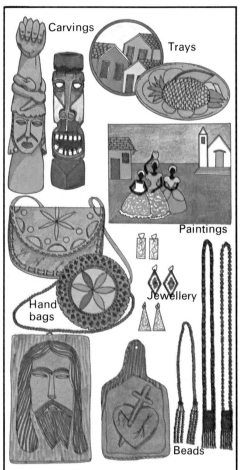

▲ Local crafts still flourish in most parts of Brazil. The woodcarvers above are from Bahia, a state where lace-making, leatherworking and gold working are also practised. Bahia is especially famous for the carving of figas (lucky charms). Further north, folk pottery is still made by the Indian method, without the use of a wheel.

▲ The cathedral of Brasilia was designed by Oscar Niemeyer. The design represents a vast crown of thorns, with curved and pointed concrete ribs supporting the glass walls and rising above the roof. The entrance to the cathedral is underground and Mass is celebrated beneath the 'tent' of glass and concrete.

▼ By contrast, the church of Sao Francisco de Assis in the goldmining town of Ouro Preto is one of the finest examples of Aleijadinho's work.

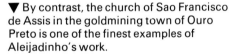

▼ Oscar Niemeyer, the architect for the government buildings in Brasilia, studied under Lucio Costa and Le Corbusier. His first major independent commission was the plan for Pampulha, a new suburb of Belo Horizonte, in 1941. Since the completion of Brasilia, Niemeyer has lived in Israel and Paris. Much of his more recent work has been in France.

A land of plenty

Agricultural diversity

Brazil is essentially an agricultural country, despite recent industrialization, and farm products account for nearly three quarters of all exports. Unlike the old days, however, the country is no longer reliant on a single crop or commodity. A tremendous range of crops is grown in the different regions and Brazil is now virtually self-sufficient in food.

Apart from coffee, major crops include sugar, rice, maize, soya-beans, wheat, cotton, tobacco and cocoa. Fruits of all kinds are grown extensively and there is a flourishing wine industry in the south – some of it is even exported to France!

Animal farming is another important branch of agriculture, especially cattle raising. The home of the *vaqueiros* in the *sertao* (the area in the north-east around the Sao Francisco river) is in decline but there are huge beef cattle ranches in Amazonas, the Mato Grosso, Sao Paulo and Goias while Minas Gerais is a centre for dairy farming. In Rio Grande do Sul the *gauchos*, the cowboys of the south, are still a common sight and often wear traditional costume.

Although there are many large *fazendas*, plantations and ranches, there are even more small farms where agricultural techniques are backward. Fertilizers and machinery are seldom used on them and subsistence farming is a way of life for thousands

▲ Like the *bandeirantes*, the *vaqueiros* of the north-east played an important role in the early expansion of Brazil. Pushing far into the sertao in their search for grazing land, they had built up a thriving cattle industry by the 17th century. Most Brazilian beef now comes from cattle crossed with hardy Zebu stock brought from India and able to cope with the sub-tropical climate. Pedigree herds are restricted to improved pastures in some of the southern states.

▶ Although Brazil produces a third of the world's coffee, annual production has declined considerably. In the 1960's the government began a programme to destroy half the country's coffee trees mainly on the poorer soils of Espirito Santo, Minas Gerais and Parana, and to encourage other types of agriculture. Frost, heavy rains and coffee rust have further reduced production in recent years but, as the drying beans prove, there is still an awful lot of coffee in Brazil!

of smallholders.

Nevertheless, if the soils of Amazonia are fertile and government incentives for modernization are a success, it may not be long before Brazil becomes a leading exporter of foodstuffs.

King Coffee

The days when coffee accounted for two-thirds or more of total Brazilian exports are gone for ever but it remains the single most important cash crop. Introduced into the north and north-east in the early eighteenth century, coffee did not become really important for another 100 years, by which time the centre of production had shifted south. Between 1850 and 1950 there were years when Brazil grew over three quarters of the world's supply of coffee and it is still the world's largest producing nation.

The rich reddish earth of Sao Paulo state was the main centre of the coffee boom and there are *fazendas* (plantations) there today. However, there was much overcropping and the leading coffee area is now in the neighbouring state of Parana. Santos, Paranagua and Rio are the chief outlets for coffee exports.

Coffee is not merely grown for overseas markets. Brazilians consume enormous quantities of coffee themselves and for many people the day would not be complete without their *cafezinhos*.

▲ Cacao, from which chocolate is made, originally grew wild in the Amazon forests but is now mainly grown in plantations in Bahia, centred around the port of Ilheus. For a time it seemed as though cacao would become as important to Brazil as coffee was but competition from West Africa prevented this.

▼ The man below is preparing the soil for an experimental variety of coffee plant. Brazil has become a centre of research into tropical agriculture and many new agricultural colleges have been established. The government is officially encouraging agrarian reform, especially the use of fertilizers and of improved farming techniques.

Brazil and the world

A colony no longer

Although political independence was achieved in 1822, separation from Portugal did not mark the end of economic colonialism in Brazil. While the colony remained under its control, the Portuguese monarchy exploited Brazil for its benefit. During the Empire and the early years of the Republic Portugal's role was assumed by Great Britain, the United States and other industrialized nations.

Brazil was little more than a tropical treasure house, providing commodities like sugar, cocoa, precious stones, cotton, rubber and coffee. She was almost totally reliant on outside sources for ideas, innovations and manufactured goods. The country had a 'boom and bust' economy which was at the mercy of its foreign trading partners.

Hardly surprisingly, Brazilians developed what amounted to a national inferiority complex. They automatically assumed that anything they manufactured for themselves would be unable to match the standards of Europe and North America.

New horizons

Only since World War II has this colonial mentality finally been buried. The government has at last begun to think of what is best for Brazil itself and economic success has been reflected in many other fields. Brazilians now realize that they have far more to offer than a few cash crops and mineral ores.

In science, the work of the Instituto Butantan in Sao Paulo on snake serums and the Instituto Oswaldo Crux in Rio de Janeiro on tropical diseases has international significance. In agriculture, the results of Brazilian research have benefited other developing nations in South America, Africa and Asia.

In the arts, figures like Portinari, Villa-Lobos and Niemeyer have earned worldwide acclaim, as have Brazilian sportsmen and women like Pele, Bueno and Fittipaldi. For over 450 years Brazilians have been responding to outside influences. Now it is Brazil's turn to export something other than coffee in exchange.

▲ President Geisel with Queen Elizabeth II during his visit to Britain in 1976. This signified far more than an exchange of diplomatic pleasantries between two heads of state. Now Brazil is beginning to flex its economic muscles and many countries are eager to conclude trade agreements. This was the main reason for the President's visit.

▼ Until 1910 Brazil was virtually the sole source of rubber for Europe and North America. The boom was centred on Manaus and huge fortunes were made until plantations were established in Malaya. Today Brazilian rubber output is insignificant on the world market, but *seringueiros* still tap wild rubber trees.

▼ Heitor Villa-Lobos (1887-1959) was a Brazilian composer with an international reputation. In his youth he was fascinated by Brazilian folk music, especially that of the north-east. He also studied the works of Bach, Puccini, Wagner and other classical composers and it was his combination of the two musical styles which made him South America's greatest composer. His output, which included operas, symphonies, concerts and solo pieces, was remarkable.

▲ The Brazilian Indians had discovered the hammock long before Europeans discovered America. Many a Brazilian still enjoys a siesta in one and in Ceara, hammock-making is a local industry. Now hammocks are used all over the world.

▼ Although coffee no longer dominates exports to the same extent, Brazil remains the world's leading producer.

▲ The roads which are being built in the Brazilian interior have international as well as domestic significance. Previously, Brazil had few road links with her Latin-American neighbours except in the extreme south. It is hoped that the new highways will not only give an economic boost to backward areas of Brazil but link with road systems in bordering countries such as Peru and Venezuela.

51

Nation of the future

Development of the Brazilian interior

Macapa
Manaus
Porto Velho
Cuiaba
Brasilia
S.Luis
Fortaleza
Natal
J.Pessoa
Recife
Maceio
Aracaju
Salvador
Vitoria
Rio de Janeiro
Curitiba
Florianopolis
Porto Alegre

International links

KEY
Roads 1964
Roads 1974
Under construction

▲ One of the greatest advances in recent years has been the opening up of the Brazilian interior. Before the building of Brasilia, the road network was concentrated around the coast and the main urban centres. Since 1960 thousands of kilometres of new roads have been built, often through virgin forest. As a result, development of the most backward areas of the country has begun. An international link will also shortly be completed. This will make it possible to travel by road from Brasilia, or any other point in Brazil, to Canada, via the Pan American highway.

Immense potential

In 1971 Brazil had the fastest economic growth rate in the world. Brazilians were already talking of their country as the Japan of Latin America, eagerly looking forward to the day when Brazil would take her place with the industrial powers.

There appeared to be every justification for their optimism. Manufactured goods now accounted for a quarter of total exports and the industrial sector was expanding at over 13 per cent a year. New roads were opening up vast areas of land for development. Huge mineral deposits had been discovered in the interior and Brazil was already a major exporter of iron ore and manganese.

Developing the nation's resources

PETROBRAS, the state oil company, was developing new fields in Sergipe and off the coast to supplement the Bahian fields and was aiming at self-sufficiency in oil by the 1980's. The hydro-electric plant at Jupia had become the nation's first, with an output of more than one million kilowatts and even larger hydro-electric schemes were under construction.

Then came the increases in the cost of imported oil and a world recession. This limited markets for Brazilian exports and some of these hopes were dimmed. People realized that there was no short-cut to industrialization and that many problems would first have to be solved. Even so, the potential is still there. With her immense resources Brazil has a firm basis on which to build herself into a major industrial power.

Unequal distribution of wealth

One of the main problems facing Brazil is that of social and economic inequality. The central and southern states are prosperous while the northern and eastern states remain economically backward, despite the work of government agencies like SUDENE and INCRA. There is similar inequality at an individual level. In the *favelas*, or slums, the drought area of the north-east and much of the interior, millions of Brazilians still live in utter poverty.

Brazilians are well aware that the key to the nation's future lies in investment in its people. New industrial plants are important but social and educational programmes are equally vital. Until Brazil has solved the problem of its poor it cannot hope to achieve its economic ambitions.

▲ The Via Anchieta is not only one of the best roads in Brazil, it is one of the most important. It links Sao Paulo with the port of Santos.

▶ Car manufacturing has enjoyed the most spectacular growth of all industries. Nearly one million cars are made annually, many of them Volkswagens.

▲ Education has a significant role to play in the country's future. The poster advertises the national campaign for literacy. At present there are still 20 million Brazilians who are unable to read or write.

▼ As cheap hydro-electric power was readily available, many industries started in Sao Paulo and it is now the largest manufacturing centre in South America. The 'Made in Brazil' label on goods for export often means 'Made in Sao Paulo'.

▲ Brazil's population explosion has led to a boom in the construction industry. Here new flats are being built in the city of Salvador.

Reference
Geography and Government

Annual rainfall of Brazil

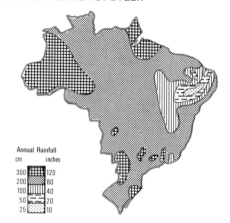

Annual Rainfall

cm	inches
300	120
200	80
100	40
50	20
25	10

Climate

Brazil is a tropical country with no real extremes of temperature. In the Amazon region the difference between the hottest and coldest months is only 5°C and in Rio it is 9°C. The range increases further south and in Rio Grande do Sul there may be frosts in winter. Temperatures are generally lower on the higher ground.

Over most of the country rainfall is moderate, although there is very heavy rainfall in parts of the Amazon basin and on the coastal escarpment. In the north-east rainfall is lower and the recurring droughts have made it one of the most depressed areas of Brazil. Most rain falls in summer, with the winters being much drier.

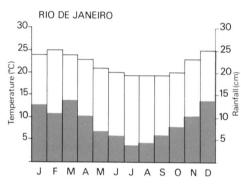

RIO DE JANEIRO

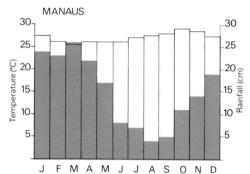

MANAUS

Natural vegetation

Forest Vegetation

- Selvas Equatorial Forest
- Montane Tropical Forest
- Catinga Xerophilous Forest
- Cerrados Sub-tropical Forest
- Cerrados Forest & Marsh
- Chaco Woodland & Savanna

Grass Vegetation

- Tropical Grassland
- Tropical Grassland & Marsh
- Sub-tropical & Temperate Grassland (Campos)

Population distribution

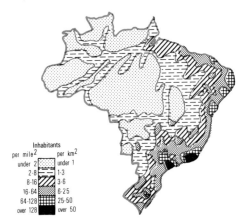

Inhabitants

per mile²	per km²
under 2	under 1
2-8	1-3
8-16	3-6
16-64	6-25
64-128	25-50
over 128	over 50

Population of Brazil

Brazil has half the total population of South America and it is growing rapidly. The density for the country as a whole is 30 to the square mile but, as the map shows, distribution is unequal.

The bulk of the population lives in the eastern third of the country with huge areas of the north and west almost uninhabited. The most heavily populated states are Sao Paulo, Rio de Janeiro and Guanabara and in the Federal District around Brasilia.

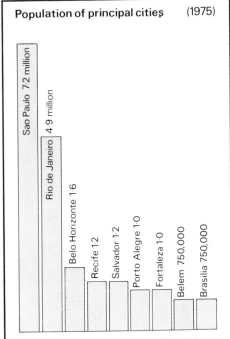

Population of principal cities   (1975)

Sao Paulo 7·2 million
Rio de Janeiro 4·9 million
Belo Horizonte 1·6
Recife 1·2
Salvador 1·2
Porto Alegre 1·0
Fortaleza 1·0
Belem 750,000
Brasilia 750,000

There are more than 60 Brazilian cities with a population of 100,000 or more. Sao Paulo, with a metropolitan population of over 10 million, is the 9th largest city in the world.

Government and administration

Each state in Brazil has its own laws and constitution within the framework of the federal constitution, and the government has the right to intervene on specific matters. The state assemblies are elected by popular vote and the assemblies in turn elect the state governors. All the states and territories are subdivided into municipalities and districts. These all have their own *prefeitos* and councils.

The National Congress comprises the Chamber of Deputies and the Senate and has legislative powers, subject to the approval of the President. The Chamber of Deputies is elected by universal suffrage and contains representatives of all the states and territories. Each state elects three Senators who remain in office for eight years.

In recent years the President's executive powers have increased at the expense of Congress. Since 1964 the President has been elected by indirect suffrage, being selected by members of Congress and representatives of the states. He serves for four years and has wide powers, especially over finance and the economy. Since 1965, all Presidents have been chosen by the National Renewal Alliance party (ARENA). The official opposition party is the Brazilian Democratic Movement (MDS).

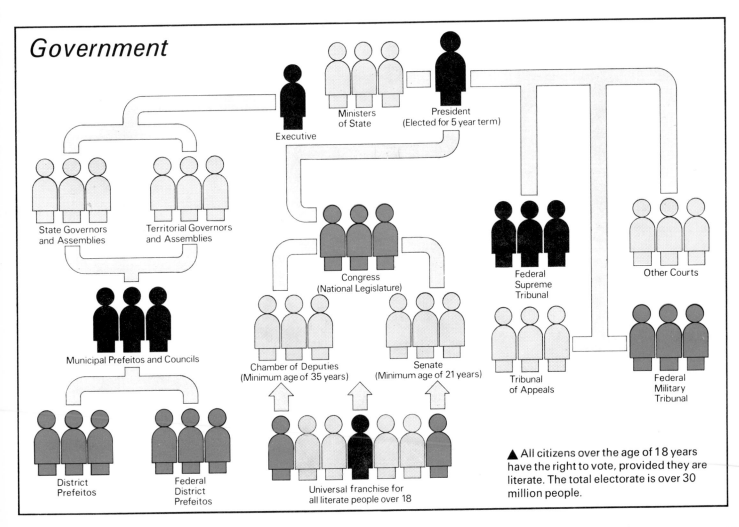

Government

Executive

Ministers of State

President (Elected for 5 year term)

State Governors and Assemblies

Territorial Governors and Assemblies

Municipal Prefeitos and Councils

District Prefeitos

Federal District Prefeitos

Congress (National Legislature)

Chamber of Deputies (Minimum age of 35 years)

Senate (Minimum age of 21 years)

Universal franchise for all literate people over 18

Federal Supreme Tribunal

Tribunal of Appeals

Other Courts

Federal Military Tribunal

▲ All citizens over the age of 18 years have the right to vote, provided they are literate. The total electorate is over 30 million people.

55

Reference
History

A.D.

pre-1500 Scattered Indian tribes were the sole inhabitants of Brazil.

1494 The Treaty of Tordesillas. South America was not yet discovered but this treaty later gave Portugal a legal claim to the coast of Brazil.

The Colonial Period

1500 Pedro Alvares Cabral landed in what is now the state of Bahia and claimed the new land for Portugal.

1501-1530 Exploration of the coast. The dyewood trade starts. Little development.

1532 First Portuguese settlement established at Sao Vicente.

1534 Brazil is divided into twelve hereditary captaincies.

1538 The first shipment of negro slaves is brought to Brazil.

1549 The first Jesuits arrive in Brazil. City of Salvador founded and becomes the seat of the Governor-General.

1551 Bishopric of Brazil created.

1553 Jesuits found a mission on the site of modern Sao Paulo.

1555-1567 Struggle between Portuguese and French for control of Guanabara Bay. Rio de Janeiro founded.

1580 Philip II of Spain unites the Spanish and Portuguese crowns.

c. 1600 The first *bandeirante* expeditions.

1612-1616 Struggle to oust French, English and Dutch from Brazil.

1624 Dutch attack on Bahia.

1630-1632 Dutch capture Recife and Olinda.

1637-1639 Pedro Teixeira's expedition to the Amazon. Claims the Amazon basin for Portugal.

1640 Joao IV restores the Portuguese monarchy. The first Viceroy to Brazil appointed.

1654 The Dutch finally expelled from Brazil.

1658 The first permanent settlement in Santa Catarina founded at Sao Francisco do Sul.

1680 *Bandeirantes* reach the River Plate and the struggle with Spain for control of Uruguay begins.

1690-1730 Gold and diamond mining towns founded in Minas Gerais, Goias and the Mato Grosso.

1750 The Treaty of Madrid between Spain and Portugal settles boundary disputes in Brazil.

1754 The captaincies are abolished.

1759 The Jesuits are expelled from Brazil.

1763 The capital is transferred from Salvador to Rio de Janeiro.

1777 The Treaty of San Ildefonso roughly fixes the boundaries of modern Brazil.

1789-1792 Unsuccessful conspiracy to establish a republic in Minas. Its leader, Tiradentes, executed.

1808 Portuguese court moved to Rio from Lisbon. Brazilian ports opened to ships of friendly nations.

1810 Preferential trading rights granted to Great Britain.

1815 Brazil given equal status with Portugal.

1821 Joao VI returns to Portugal, leaving Dom Pedro as Regent. Uruguay incorporated into Brazil as Cisplatine Province.

The Empire

1822 Declaration of Independence. The Regent becomes Emperor Pedro I.

1824 The first Brazilian constitution.

1825-1828 War with Argentina. Uruguay established as a Republic.

1831 Pedro I abdicates in favour of his five-year-old son.

1831-1840 Brazil ruled by the Regency. General unrest.

1840 Pedro II is proclaimed Emperor.

1844 Dispute with Great Britain over the continuation of the slave trade to Brazil.

1850 Law abolishing the African slave trade.

1865-1870 The War of the Triple Alliance. Brazil, Argentina and Uruguay win costly struggle with Paraguay.

1871 Law providing for gradual abolition of slavery in Brazil.

1885 All slaves over 60 freed.

1888 Final abolition of slavery.

The Republic

1889 Pedro II forced to abdicate. The Republic is declared, November 15.

1891 First Republican constitution. Deodoro da Fonseca becomes Provisional President but is later forced to resign.

1893-1895 Civil war which is eventually won by government.

1894 Prudente de Morais is elected the first civilian President.

1917 Brazil enters World War I on the side of the allies.

1922 Military unrest leads to revolt in Rio de Janeiro.

1924 Military uprising in Sao Paulo.

1924-1927 The Prestes Column marches through the interior but fails to start a popular revolution.

1929 World depression leads to disastrous fall in coffee prices.

1930 Getulio Vargas defeated in the Presidential elections but seizes power.

1932 Revolt in Sao Paulo suppressed.

1934 New constitution. Vargas elected President by Congress.

1937 *Estado Novo* (New State) established with Vargas as dictator.

1942 Brazil joins Allies in World War II.

1944 Brazilian army takes part in the Italian campaign.

1945 Bloodless military coup removes Vargas from power. War Minister General Dutra elected President.

1946 Fourth Constitution of the Republic.

1950 Vargas is re-elected President.

1954 Vargas forced to resign. Commits suicide.

1956 Juscelino Kubitschek elected President.

1960 The capital is transferred from Rio to Brasilia.

1961 Constitutional crisis. Joao Goulart becomes President with reduced powers.

1963 A plebiscite restores the Presidential system of government.

1964 The mounting economic crisis and the President's radical views lead to a military revolt deposing Goulart. The First Institutional Act legalizes the new regime. Marshal Humberto Castelo Branco elected interim President.

1965 The Second Institutional Act disbands the existing political parties.

1967 The Fifth Constitution of the Republic grants more power to the central government.

1968 Mounting political unrest prompts President Costa e Silva to assume emergency powers.

1968-1974 Economic recovery and impressive industrial growth.

1974 General Ernesto Geisel becomes President. Grants amnesty to the regime's political opponents.

1975 After surprise victories by the opposition parties in congressional elections, Geisel declares his determination to retain emergency powers.

The Arts

ARCHITECTURE AND SCULPTURE

Colonial architecture was dominated by Portuguese influences which were adapted to a tropical environment. In more recent years Brazil has evolved its own styles, and architecture is one of the country's most flourishing art forms. Brasilia is the best example of this but there are many other fine modern buildings such as the Museum of Modern Art in Rio, the church of Pampulha in Belo Horizonte and the development at Pedregulho.

Brazilian sculpture also developed under strong Portuguese influence, as is shown by the decoration of the colonial churches of Salvador. Modern sculpture came to the fore in the 1920's in a movement which produced sculptors such as Maria Martins and Sergio Camargo. However, it is still one of the most neglected artistic disciplines.

Lisboa, Antonio Francisco (1738-1814). Better known as *O Aleijadinho*, the Little Cripple. A prolific and influential sculptor and architect in Minas Gerais, he designed and decorated the sanctuary of Bom Jesus de Matozinhos at Congonhas do Campo and the church of Sao Francisco in Ouro Preto. Despite his deformities, he worked until his death.
Costa, Lucio (1902–). Born in France, he is an architect best known for creating the master plan of Brasilia. He also helped to design the Ministry of Education and Health building in Rio.
Niemeyer (Soares Filho), Oscar (1907–). Also worked on the Ministry of Education building. He designed the government buildings in Brasilia and has built many other fine modern churches and public buildings in Brazil and Europe.
Burle Marx, Roberto (1909–). A landscape architect, he designed many beautiful gardens, notably the one at Odette Monteiro House near Rio. He also designed the street mosaic on Rio's Avenida Atlantica.
Reidy, Affonso Eduardo (1909-1964). Another of the team on the Ministry of Education building. His most admired works include the Pedregulho development and the Museum of Modern Art in Rio.

PAINTING

A French art mission in 1816 gave an impetus to Brazilian painting but for many years there was no national style. In the 1920's, however, many young Europeans came to settle in Brazil. Lazar Segal, a Russian by birth, was the first to start expressing the Brazilian character on canvas and he was followed by Guignard, Ibere Camargo, Milton da Costa, Manabu Mabe and many others.

A flourishing school of engraving also emerged led by Ostrower, Roberto de Lamonica and Maria Bonomi. There is also a school of primitive painters whose work depicts Brazilian regional life.

Segal, Lazar (1890–). An expressionist, born in Russia. His paintings, such as *Eternos Caminhantes*, reflect Brazilian moods and themes.
Cavalcanti, Emiliano Di (1897–). The most famous living Brazilian painter. His paintings, murals and posters deal mainly with the Brazilian people and countryside.
Portinari, Candido (1903-1962). Brazil's best known artist internationally. His murals and paintings translate the life of ordinary people into dramatic and powerful pictures. His mural on war and peace decorates the United Nations Building in New York.

LITERATURE

There are four main periods in Brazilian literature – the colonial, the romantic, the post-romantic and the modernist.

Matos Guerra, Gregorio De (1633-1696). The most colourful figure in early Brazilian literature. His caustic verses earned him the nickname 'the devil's mouthpiece'. No single great poem but the first real Brazilian poet.
Goncalves Dias, Antonio (1823-1864). The national poet of Brazil and compiler of a Tupi-Portuguese dictionary. A Romantic, many of his poems extolled the Indians. Most famous for his *Song of Exile.*
Alencar, Jose Martiniano De (1829-1877). A Romantic novelist who dealt mainly with Indians and frontier life. *O Guarani, Iracema* and *O Gaucho.*
Almeida, Manuel Antonio De (1831-1861). The author of the first great Brazilian novel, *Memoirs of a Militia Sergeant.*
Machado De Assis, Joaquim (1839-1908). Poet, novelist and short story writer, he is the greatest figure in Brazilian literature and his works portray society during the Empire. His masterpiece was *Dom Casmurro.* Also *Braz Cubas* and *Quincas Borba.*
Castro Alves, Antonio De (1847-1871). Called the poet of the slaves because of his demands for their freedom. *Espumas Flutuantes* and *De Escravos.*
Azevedo, Aluizio De (1857-1913). Naturalistic novelist who modelled himself on Zola. *O Mulato* and *Casa de Pensao.*
Cunha, Euclides Da (1866-1909). A novelist whose *Os Sertoes (Rebellion in the Backlands)* is considered to be Brazil's greatest single prose work.
Bandeira, Manuel (1886-1968). The leading Brazilian poet of his age. *A Cinza das Horas, Libertinagem* and *Estrela de Manha.*
Almeida, Jose Americo de (1897–). The first of the north-eastern regional novelists. *A Bagaceira.*

Andrade, Mario de (1893-1945). Novelist and poet. *Macunaima* and *Hallucinated City.*
Meireles, Cecelia (1901-1964). Lyrical poet. *Obra Poetica.*
Drummond de Andrade, Carlos (1902–). The greatest living Brazilian poet. *Alguma Poesia* was his first major collection.
Guimaraes Rosa, Joao (1908-1967). Unconventional modern novelist. *The Devil to Pay in the Backlands.*
Queiroz, Rachel de (1910–). The most esteemed woman novelist in Brazil. Deals with the North-east. *The Three Marias, Caminho de Pedras.*
Amado, Jorge (1912). Another writer from the North-east and Brazil's best known living novelist. Translated into 33 different languages. *Gabriela, Cravo e Canela* is his most famous work.

MUSIC

Brazil is best known for its popular music such as the samba and bossa nova.

Mauricio, Fray Jose (1767-1830). Composer of religious music. *Requiem Mass in B Flat.*
Gomes, Carlos (1836-1896). Composer of operas in the Italian style. *Il Guarany* and *Lo Schiavo.*
Villa-Lobos, Heitor (1887-1959). The foremost 20th-century South American composer. Most of his 1,700 works adapted traditional melodies and rhythms into symphonic forms. His *Bachianas Brasileiras* is perhaps his best known work.

THEATRE AND CINEMA

Brazil has no great theatrical tradition, although in the last 40 years playwrights like Nelson Rodrigues and Ariano Suassuna have earned themselves a national reputation.

The cinema, however, has flourished in Brazil since the silent era and Mario Peixoto, Alberto Cavalcanti, Anselmo Duarte and Nelson Pereira dos Santos have all won international awards for their films.

Guide to pronunciation
Brazilian Portuguese bears the same relationship to European Portuguese as American does to English – it is not so formal and some of the pronunciations are simplified. Even so, the nasal sounds make it a difficult language for foreigners to speak correctly.

There are four written accents (acute, circumflex, grave and til) and the penultimate or last syllable is generally stressed. Brazilians tend to speak very fast and to run their words together so one of the most useful phrases for a beginner is *Por favor, fale mais devagar!* (Please speak more slowly.)

Reference
The Economy

Agriculture in Brazil

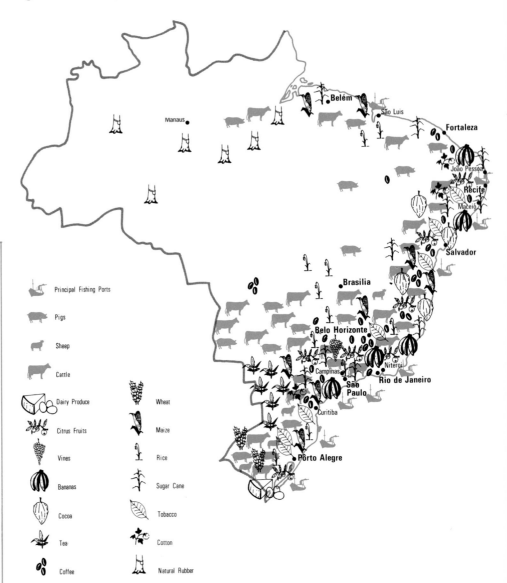

Map legend
- Principal Fishing Ports
- Pigs
- Sheep
- Cattle
- Dairy Produce
- Citrus Fruits
- Vines
- Bananas
- Cocoa
- Tea
- Coffee
- Wheat
- Maize
- Rice
- Sugar Cane
- Tobacco
- Cotton
- Natural Rubber

FACTS AND FIGURES

Gross National Product (1975):
880.530 million cruzeiros.

Economic growth rate: Between
1968 and 1974 the total growth of the
economy was 50 per cent. Since then
the rate has dropped slightly.

Inflation: (1975) 20-30 per cent.

Cost of living: (1970=100) May,
1975=249.

Main trading partners: The USA
provides more than 25 per cent of
imports and takes approximately 20
per cent of exports. Other main trading
partners are the EEC, Japan and
LAFTA.

Main sources of income:

Agriculture: Brazil is the world's
largest producer and exporter of coffee
and cane sugar. It ranks 3rd among
cocoa producers, 4th in tobacco and
5th in cotton. Other leading crops are
maize, rice, edible beans, cassava,
wheat, bananas, oranges, soya beans
and grapes. There are over 100 million
cattle, 70 million pigs and 40 million
sheep and goats.

Forest: Brazil has immense stands of
both hard and softwoods and pine-
wood is an important export. Other
forest products are rubber, brazil and
cashew nuts, and waxes.

Fishing: Output has doubled over the
past 20 years but fishing remains a
relatively insignificant sector of the
economy.

Mining: Mineral resources are vast
and generally undeveloped. They
include iron ore, manganese, bauxite,
asbestos, nickel, uranium, tin, zinc,
and gemstones.

Industry: Iron and steel, petro-
chemicals, cars (10th largest in world),
shipbuilding, textiles, tobacco, cement.

Energy: Brazil has tremendous hydro-
electric power potential. It produces
some natural gas and low-grade coal.
It hopes to be self-sufficient in oil by
the 1980's.

Economic standing

Brazilian potential is as yet largely unexploited
but Brazil is a significant source of primary
products. It is the world's leading producer of
coffee, bananas and beans. It also ranks
among the top five producers of asbestos,
cattle, cocoa, corn, cotton, manganese,
sugar and tobacco. More important for the
future are the resources which have not so
far been developed – the vast deposits of
iron ore and other minerals, the uncut timber,
the millions of acres of fertile soil and the
immense hydro-electric potential.

Slowly but surely the country is making
full use of its riches and in the early 1970's it
had one of the fastest expanding economies
in the world with an annual growth rate of
9 per cent. More recently this has slowed
down, however. Although much of the
interior remains a wilderness, Brazil is
already becoming one of the world's larger
manufacturing nations.

Agriculture

This is the most important sector of the
economy, employing over 40 per cent of the
workforce and accounting for nearly 75 per
cent of exports. In many areas methods of
production are backward and the
agricultural heartland is in Sao Paulo, Minas
Gerais and the three southern states where
more use is made of fertilizer, machinery and
advanced techniques.

Coffee is the main crop for export but
production is falling, as is that of cocoa. On
the other hand, cotton, sugar, rice and corn
output has increased considerably. Apart
from its exports, Brazil is virtually self-
sufficient in basic foodstuffs.

Livestock, especially beef and dairy cattle,
accounts for one third of agricultural output
but the rich fishing grounds off the coast are
inefficiently exploited. Brazil's timber
resources are vast, but much of the timber
is inaccessible at the moment.

Industry

This is the most dynamic sector of the economy. From 1947 to 1961 annual growth ran at 10 per cent and it returned to this level in the late '60's and early '70's. Manufactured goods now account for more than a quarter of the gross domestic product, although they have a relatively small part of the export trade. One major problem is that of imbalance — two-thirds of all industrial production is concentrated in the Sao Paulo area.

The industrial base rests mainly on iron and steel, motor vehicles, shipbuilding and the petrochemical industry. Shipbuilding is already an important source of exports but the most spectacular growth has occurred in the car industry — Brazil is the largest producer in South America. Other major industries are textiles, cement, tobacco, and chemicals.

Mining

Although new mineral deposits are being discovered all the time, exploitation is at an early stage. Iron ore (mostly from Minas Gerais) and manganese (80 per cent from Amapa) are most important but considerable amounts of bauxite, apatite, dolomite, gem stones, diamonds, lead, tin, chromite and asbestos are also mined.

About 40 per cent of Brazil's oil is produced nationally and the discovery of new fields gives hope for self-sufficiency. Unfortunately, most of Brazil's coal is of poor quality.

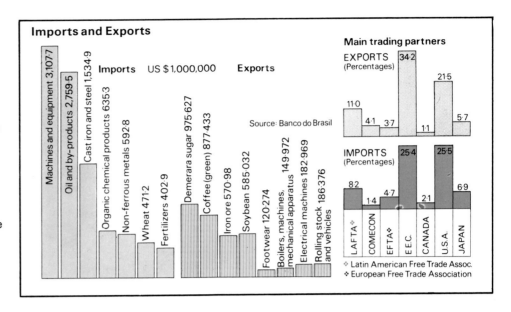

Imports and Exports

Imports   US $1,000,000   Exports

Machines and equipment 3,107·7
Oil and by-products 2,759·5
Cast iron and steel 1,534·9
Organic chemical products 635·3
Non-ferrous metals 592·8
Wheat 471·2
Fertilizers 402·9

Demerara sugar 975·627
Coffee (green) 877·433
Iron ore 570·98
Soybean 585·032
Footwear 120·274
Boilers, machines, mechanical apparatus 149·972
Electrical machines 182·969
Rolling stock and vehicles 186·376

Source: Banco do Brasil

Main trading partners

EXPORTS (Percentages)

LAFTA	COMECON	EFTA	E.E.C.	CANADA	U.S.A.	JAPAN
11·0	4·1	3·7	34·2	1·1	21·5	5·7

IMPORTS (Percentages)

LAFTA	COMECON	EFTA	E.E.C.	CANADA	U.S.A.	JAPAN
8·2	1·4	4·7	25·4	2·1	25·5	6·9

✧ Latin American Free Trade Assoc.
✧ European Free Trade Association

Industry in Brazil

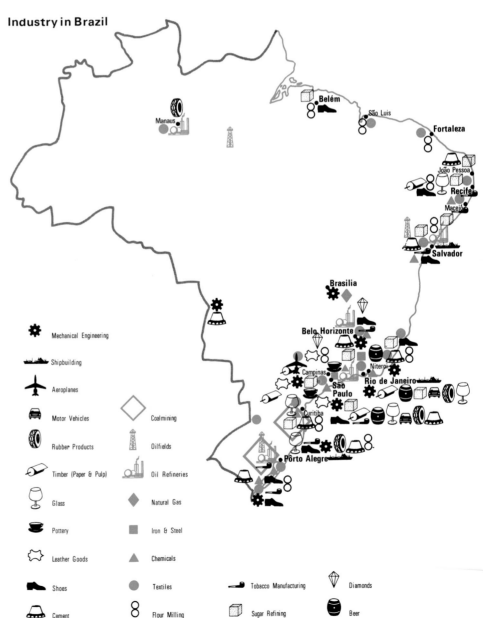

Mechanical Engineering
Shipbuilding
Aeroplanes
Motor Vehicles   Coalmining
Rubber Products   Oilfields
Timber (Paper & Pulp)   Oil Refineries
Glass   Natural Gas
Pottery   Iron & Steel
Leather Goods   Chemicals
Shoes   Textiles
Cement   Flour Milling

Tobacco Manufacturing   Diamonds
Sugar Refining   Beer

Division of labour

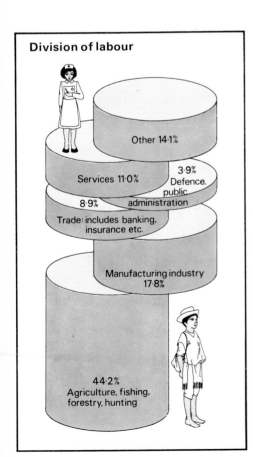

Other 14·1%

Services 11·0%

3·9% Defence, public administration

8·9% Trade: includes banking, insurance etc.

Manufacturing industry 17·8%

44·2% Agriculture, fishing, forestry, hunting

Gazetteer

Population figures quoted are 1970 census.

Acre (9 00S 70 00W) Northern state. Mainly forest covered. Produces best rubber in Brazil. Capital: Rio Branco. Area: 152,531 sq. kms. Pop: 218,000.

Alagoas (9 00S 36 00W) North-eastern agricultural state. Sugar, cotton, tobacco, cattle, rice, corn. Produces some oil. Sugar refining main industry. Capital: Maceio (243,000). Area: 27,720 sq. kms. Pop: 1,606,000.

Amapa (1 00N 52 00W) Northern territory. Manganese, timber, rubber. Capital: Macapa. Area: 140,223 sq. kms. Pop: 116,000.

Amazon (0 05S 50 00W) Second longest river in the world at 6,275 kms. Drains almost half of Brazil. A major route into the interior. Its basin only sparsely populated.

Amazonas (4 00S 64 00W) Largest state. Mainly forested. Rubber, brazil nuts, timber, jute. Believed to have rich mineral reserves. Capital: Manaus. Area: 1,563,849 sq. kms. Pop: 961,000.

Bahia (11 00S 42 00W) Eastern coastal state produces 85 per cent of Brazil's oil and various other minerals. Agriculture — cacao, tobacco, sugar, cattle. Some industry. Great hydro-electric potential. Capital: Salvador. Area: 560,811 sq. kms. Pop: 7,583,000.

Belem (1 27S 48 29W) Main port for Amazon and largest northern city. Many fine colonial buildings. Exports timber, hides, brazil nuts, jute and forest products. Pop: 565,000.

Belo Horizonte (19 55S 43 56W) Capital and focus of mining industry in Minas Gerais. A major agricultural and industrial centre. Pop: 1,235,000.

Brasilia (16 12S 44 26W) The federal capital and a national symbol. Inauguration in 1960 marked beginning of drive to open up the interior. Noted for its striking modern architecture. Pop: 495,000.

Ceara (5 00S 40 00W) Primarily agricultural north-eastern state. Cotton (3rd largest in Brazil), cattle, sugar. Home of *jangadeiros* and *vaqueiros*. Capital: Fortaleza. Area: 147,959 sq. kms. Pop: 4,492,000.

Espirito Santo (19 30S 40 30W) Small coastal state. Primarily agricultural — coffee, rice, cocoa, sugar, corn, cattle, poultry. Capital: Vitoria (136,000). Area: 45,579 sq. kms. Pop: 1,618,000.

Fortaleza (3 43S 38 30W) Capital of Ceara. A major port and commercial and cultural centre. Main exports sugar, coffee, cotton, rice, hides. Pop: 859,000.

Goias (12 00S 48 00W) An inland state, part of rapidly developing interior.

Agriculture and livestock most important economically. Minerals include gold, diamonds, titanium, tin. Capital: Goiania (362,000). Area: 641,790 sq. kms. Pop: 2,998,000.

Iguacu Falls (25 41S 54 26W) Waterfall on Argentinian border. 4 kms. wide and 89 metres high. One of South America's main tourist attractions.

Manaus (3 08S 60 01W) River port and capital of Amazonas. Agricultural and commercial centre. Was focus of rubber boom. Now a free port and tourist centre. Pop: 303,000.

Maranhao (5 00S 45 00W) Northern state. Low, heavily-forested region bordered by the Atlantic. Largely dependent on agriculture and livestock. Has undeveloped bauxite and oil resources. Capital: Sao Luis (168,000). Area: 328,536 sq. kms. Pop: 3,037,000.

Mato Grosso (16 00S 56 00W) One of the least developed interior states. Much cattle raising. Coffee in south. Rich mineral deposits (gold, diamonds, iron, manganese, nickel, platinum). Capital: Cuiaba (84,000). Area: 1,231,080 sq. kms. Pop: 1,624,000.

Minas Gerais (18 00S 44 00W) Means 'general mines' and this inland state is rich in minerals. Gold and diamonds first attracted settlers. Now vast deposits of iron ore and manganese more important. Many industries in the cities — steel, food processing, textiles, chemicals. Agriculture also very important, especially beef and dairy cattle. Capital: Belo Horizonte. Area: 586,947 sq. kms. Pop: 11,645,000.

Ouro Preto (20 23S 43 30W) Centre of 18th-century gold rush in Minas. Site of many of Aleijadinho's masterpieces. Whole city now a national monument. Pop: 24,000.

Para (4 00S 53 00W) Heavily-forested northern state. Jute, black pepper and forest products. Capital: Belem. Area: 1,227,062 sq. kms. Pop: 2,197,000.

Paraiba (7 15S 36 30W) North-eastern state. Mainly agricultural (sugar, cotton, sisal, tobacco) but some copper and tin mined. Capital: Joao Pessoa (197,000). Area: 56,350 sq. kms. Pop: 2,445,000.

Parana (24 00S 51 00W) Rich southern state. Is now main producer of coffee and also has important timber industry. Other main crops are cotton, peanuts, *mate*, corn. Many cattle and pigs. Capital: Curitiba. Area: 199,477 sq. kms. Pop: 6,998,000.

Pernambuco (8 00S 37 00W) Economically depressed north-eastern state despite work of SUDENE. In the heart of 'drought polygon'. Sugar grown near coast. Many cattle in the interior. Capital: Recife. Area: 98,245 sq. kms. Pop: 5,252,000.

Piaui (7 00S 43 00W) Another semi-arid north-eastern state. Lacks good communications. Livestock, palm oil, wax. Capital: Teresina (181,000). Area: 250,838 sq. kms. Pop: 1,735,000.

Porto Alegre (30 04S 51 11W) Major agricultural, commercial and industrial centre. The 'gaucho' capital. Meat packing, tanning, chemicals, tobacco, textiles. Pop: 886,000.

Recife (8 03S 34 48W) Regional capital for the north-east. An important agricultural and industrial centre. Pop: 1,061,000.

Rio de Janeiro (22 54S 43 15W) Major port; commercial and financial centre. Cultural and tourist 'capital' of Brazil. Second industrial city — publishing, textiles, foodstuffs, electrical goods, clothes, metallurgy. Pop: 4,252,000.

Rio de Janeiro State (22 00S 42 30W) Contains some of Brazil's highest peaks. A mixed economy with varied industries. Capital: Niteroi. Area: 42,895 sq. kms. Pop: 4,795,000.

Rio Grande do Norte (5 45S 36 00W) North-eastern state. Primarily agricultural. Produces 95 per cent of Brazil's salt. Some fishing. Capital: Natal (251,000). Area: 52,994 sq. kms. Pop: 1,612,000.

Rio Grande do Sul (30 00S 54 00W) Southernmost state, long known as granary of Brazil (rice, wheat, corn). Wines and tobacco. Many cattle — the 'gaucho' state. Industries in cities. Capital: Porto Alegre. Area: 282,077 sq. kms. Pop: 6,755,000.

Rondonia (11 00S 63 00W) Sparsely-populated forested territory. Rubber, brazil nuts. Capital: Porto Velho. Area: 242,020 sq. kms. Pop: 117,000.

Roraima (1 00S 61 00W) Territory with less than 1 person per sq. km. Capital: Boa Vista. Area: 230,017 sq. kms. Pop: 42,000.

Salvador (12 59S 38 31W) Brazil's first capital and main centre of slave trade. Famous for fine colonial churches, African folklore and highly spiced foods. A major port with varied industries. Centre of *macumba* cult (called *candomble* here). Pop: 1,008,000.

Santa Catarina (27 00S 50 00W) Southern state. Economy based mainly on timber and wood products. Coal, fishing, cattle and food processing also important. Capital: Florianapolis (116,000). Area: 95,948 sq. kms. Pop: 2,930,000.

Santos (23 57S 46 20W) Brazil's second port and largest coffee port in world. Holiday resort for Sao Paulo. Pop: 341,000.

Sao Francisco (10 30S 36 24W) Longest river wholly within Brazil (2,896 kms.).

Sao Paulo (23 32S 46 37W) Brazil's largest city and greatest industrial centre in South America. Tremendous variety in manufacturing and accounts for over 60 per cent of Brazil's total. Also a banking and cultural centre. Pop: 5,922,000.

Sao Paulo State (22 00S 49 00W) The 'powerhouse' of Brazil. Most important state for industry and agriculture and dominates Brazilian economy. Capital: Sao Paulo. Area: 247,803 sq. kms. Pop: 17,959,000.

Sergipe (10 30S 37 30W) Impoverished coastal state with few natural resources. Mainly agriculture and livestock, although oil, salt and potassium also produced. Capital: Aracaju (180,000). Area: 21,986 sq. kms. Pop: 911,000.

Volta Redonda (22 32S 44 07W) Largest steel manufacturing city in South America, producing 75 per cent of Brazilian output. Pop: 121,000.

Index

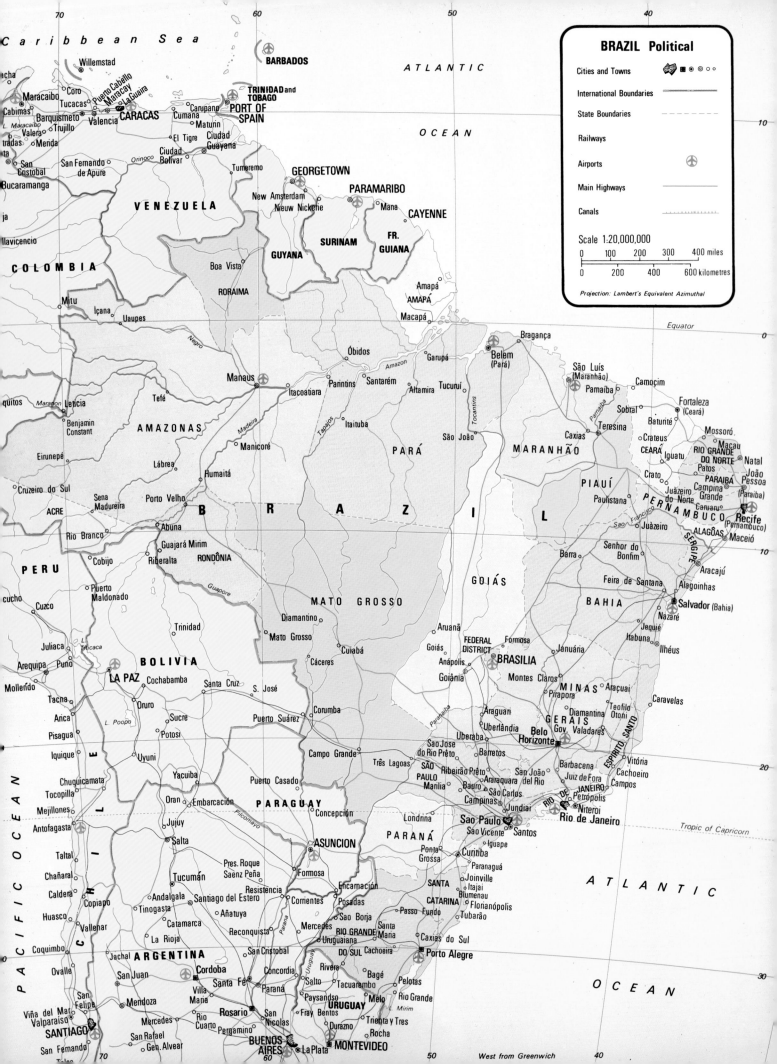

1 2 3 4 5 6 7 8 9 Cad 84 83 82 81 80 79 78